Ruins ALONG THE River

MONTEZUMA CASTLE, TUZIGOOT AND MONTEZUMA WELL NATIONAL MONUMENTS

WRITTEN BY CARLE HODGE
PHOTOGRAPHY BY GEORGE H. H. HUEY

Copyright 1986 by
Western National Parks Association
ISBN 0-911408-68-1
Library of Congress Number 86-061462
Editorial: T.J. Priehs and Carolyn Dodson
Design: McQuiston & Daughter, Inc.

Printed in Korea

C O N T E N T S

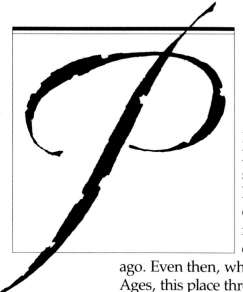

PEOPLE WITHOUT WATER
From high in the pine-clad mountains to the north, a stream born of snowmelt gushes downward through a valley that seems remarkably verdant to eyes dazzled by the desert sun. Waterways are uncommon here in the Arizona midland and where they flow, they are the very veins of existence. The Verde River differed little a thousand years ago. Even then, when Europeans had not yet fully triumphed over the Dark Ages, this place throbbed with human endeavor. Farmers in the Verde Valley already coaxed the waters of the river and its constellation of tributaries onto fields to till crops.

They had come as nomads, living precariously off the land and sleeping in caves or little more than covered trenches. Then they learned to husband beans, corns and squash, to grow and spin cotton and to construct cities of stone. Some, like Montezuma Castle, which broods above Beaver Creek, were fitted into the sheltering alcoves of cliffs. Others commanded ridge-tops, as at Tuzigoot, beside the river itself.

Weapons and utensils were fashioned from materials at hand. Nature granted wild animals for meat and wild plants for food and medicines, but also fearsome disasters that drove away entire communities. The resulting tides of migration turned the Valley into a melting pot of disparate peoples, and a kaleidoscope of ideas.

Although survival remained a constant challenge,

5

the Valley people not only endured, they created. An agrarian, sedentary society brought leisure and thus permitted for the first time the role of specialists, of priests and artisans. The artisans crafted elaborate jewelry, much of it from gemstones mined nearby, that evokes the envy of modern-day designers.

Commerce was brisk. Salt, cotton and other Valley goods were exchanged for parrots from tropical Mexico, seashells from the Gulf of California and painted pottery from the mesas to the northeast. Timed to the seasons and fueled by trade and rituals, the cycles of the stone cities persisted for more than four centuries. But now there are only ruins.

Scholars are uncertain about the origins of these prehistoric people. Equally compelling is the mystery of why they vanished a half century before Columbus landed in the Indies. Were they ravaged by war or pestilence? The Indians of the Verde were part of a cultural flowering that took place throughout the Southwest. Chaco Canyon, Mesa Verde, Casa Grande: all, like the citadels of the Verde, were abandoned by A.D. 1450.

These resolute settlers of the Valley first were recognized as a distinct culture on the higher Colorado Plateau, where moisture also is precious. It was from that milieu that an admiring archeologist derived a name for them. They were the Sinagua—in Spanish, "without water."

LEGACY OF THE LAKES

Now, cool creeks murmur under canopies of cottonwood, sycamore and velvet ash trees. But great beasts once drank here from a chain of desert lakes, against a geological backdrop already old beyond common comprehension.

Crowning the crimson cliffs to the north and east, 4,000 feet above today's Verde Valley, are rocks that were cemented in place between 240 million and 225 million years ago, before the first rudimentary animals floundered onto land. Beneath that hard, marine Kaibab limestone, bequeathed by rising and receding seas, rest softer, windborne sandstones and siltstones and finally the Supai Group, the picture-postcard red rocks of the Oak Creek country.

These were the primordial ingredients with which Nature slowly sculpted the Valley we see. Continual contortions of uplifting and tilting, then of folding and faulting, jumbled the landscape.

About 38 million years ago, the ancestral Verde River began knifing through the Kaibab and the other formations that are layered, cake-like, below it. Because pebbles from the highlands south of the Valley appear to the north on the high Colorado Plateau, scientists surmise that the Verde meandered north at that time.

Relentlessly, over millions of years, the stream scoured and sanded the surface until it had abraded a basin much like that of the present, which is 30 miles long and up to 20 miles wide. Steaming lava flows periodically spilled into the Valley from the north, flicking out the dark bands that remain across the Black Hills that shoulder the basin to the west and south. Then, the restless Earth twisted more abruptly. A seizure of faulting rent the region some

seven or eight million years ago, thrusting the Black Hills even higher. This, with the lava extrusions, dammed the river. A necklace of still waters soon glistened across a landscape where now there is little more than desert shrubs and chalky, low white hills.

Some of the lakes—the playas—often were dry. Even the more permanent bodies, rarely more than 20 feet deep, shrank and rose in response to fickle rainfall. Snails scavenged the bottoms, blanketed by fresh-water clams and the slime of dead single-celled diatoms. Turtles moved through the shallow water.

Of the animals that frequented the lakes, many were the forerunners of those that flourish here today: packrats, pocket gophers, voles, deer mice and kangaroo rats, those tiny rodents whose desert descendants hop on their hind legs and can live a lifetime without drinking water. Kangaroo rats subsist on minute amounts of so-called metabolic water, produced as their bodies process the seeds they eat. Just as it would become a meld of prehistoric peoples, the Valley attracted an assortment of animals from the cooler mountainous north and the warmer desert south.

From fossils that have been found, it has been determined that large mammals now extinct muddied the marshy shores. Camels, bears, mammoths and elephantlike gomphotheres, horses and three-toed ponies sipped from the lakes, along with meat-eaters much like jaguars, American lions and ring-tailed cats. The tracks of some, cast in stone, have been discovered near Montezuma Castle.

The Verde River, and its
numerous tributaries, provides
a verdant contrast to the
surrounding desert and was the
focal point of life for the ancient
dwellers of Montezuma Castle
and Tuzigoot.

7

Why the mammoths and many other lumbering mammals vanished somewhat suddenly, many only about 11,000 years before the present, no one is certain. While some scientists suspect they were hunted to oblivion by ancient Southwesterners, others blame climatic changes.

Not all these animals of the lakes shared the same time spans. Rather, they lived intermittently during, and some after, the millions of years the lakes lasted. About two million years ago, erosion crumbled the natural dam at the southern end of the Valley. The lakes slowly emptied, leaving only the river itself and such small streams as Beaver Creek, later to be the lifelines for the residents of Montezuma Castle and Tuzigoot. The river surged into its modern course, heading southward.

Still, the lakes left a legacy. Frequent evaporation of the playas deposited deep beds of salt that would help sustain the prehistoric people yet to come, and provide them with a profitable item for barter. Since the tributaries that nourished the lakes were rich in calcium carbonate, washed down from the Colorado Plateau, freshwater limestone had caked in the old lake beds. This limestone, the Verde Formation, is about 2,000 feet thick, surfacing as the white-striped hills that characterize the Valley and veneering the cliffs where some of the Sinagua would imbed their dwellings.

So, the planet's writhing, and the whittling by water and wind, cleaved a corridor that connected the high plateaus to the north and the basin-and-range desert to the south, a natural artery for the human travel and trade still far in the future.

DISCOVERERS AND DIGGERS

Just which of the conquistadors, fanning across the Southwest for souls and gold, initially came upon the silent villages quite likely will remain unresolved. Probably it was Antonio de Espejo who, in 1583, trudged from the Hopi mesas to the Indian copper mines in the Black Hills. If he followed Beaver Creek to the Verde River, he would have passed near Montezuma Castle. According to the journal of one of his men, the expedition chanced upon a spring or marsh "which flows into a small water ditch, and we came to an abandoned pueblo."

Few Europeans strayed into the area over the following few centuries. With the end of the Mexican War in 1848, however, the Valley became American territory and the fiefdom of trappers. Beavers thrived then in the Verde drainage. Yet the pelt-hunters were as taciturn about the ancient towns as the Spaniards had been—or equally unimpressed.

Civilization was coming closer, nonetheless. In the early 1860s, the settlers streaming into the country were not warmly welcomed by all of the Indians, a condition that led to a new calling: the Indian fighters. One, King Woolsey, made a forray into the Tonto Basin in 1864, and returning to Prescott, one of his men told a newspaper they had seen an "immense spring or well with walled caves in the cliffs surrounding it. They were probably built by the Aztecs. We gave the name of Montezuma to the well."

Montezuma never had ventured within a thousand miles of the place, of course, and the Aztecs had nothing to do with it. A year after the Woolsey visit, U.S. troops rode into the Valley to establish Fort Verde. Never truly fortified, the small encampment played an important, if scarcely cinematic, role in subduing the natives.

By 1884, when Edgar Alexander Mearns came to Fort Verde as post surgeon, central Arizona was at peace. Peace apparently was what attracted the 28-year-old physician from Highland Falls, near West Point up the Hudson River from New York City. He wished to pursue his eclectic scientific interests.

Later, he was attached to the commission that fixed the Mexican border, served the Army in the Philippines and accompanied Theodore Roosevelt on an African safari. Wherever he was, Mearns tirelessly collected the fauna, and it was during his four years at Fort Verde that he began his career as a naturalist.

While in Arizona, Mearns collected and preserved thousands of birds and animals, including a species of quail named for him. He also was the first person with scientific training to assess and report on the Valley's prehistory.

From what he called "the aboriginal monuments," he extracted "several thousand" artifacts, destined for museums in New York and Washington. Among those from Montezuma Castle was "a handsomely wrought marlinspike fashioned from the leg-bone of a deer." He also found a corn-shucker made of bone, sticks for fire making, gourd cups, sycamorewood spoons and cords of cotton and yucca. "Some oven-shaped cupboards" along one wall held bits of mescal, pinyon nuts and other food fragments. "A careless shot, aimed at the building by some passing hunter, put us in possession of an interesting relic," Mearns pointed out later; a stray bullet had dislodged a stone axe imbedded in some timbers.

In an 1890 article in *Popular Science Monthly* Mearns recounted his excavation of the cliff condominiums. He wrote that he "caused the debris on the floors to be shoveled over," the worst of the overburden being a four-foot thickness of bat guano. He also provided a wry aside on the size of the doorways: "The traveler in this region is quite certain of being entertained by exaggerated stories about gigantic human skeletons having been discovered in the ruined casas grandes; but if he be a good-sized man, and possessed of adipose tissue appertaining to the age of threescore years, he will become skeptical thereof when he comes to squeeze himself through the narrow portals of the ancient halls." One room, he recounted, had to be entered through "a window of sub-Gothic form," three-feet, three-inches high and two-feet, four-inches wide.

From the quartermaster at Fort Verde, the doctor borrowed "four substantial wooden ladders." The lowest part of what he called "this casa, doubtless a fortress" stands 42 feet above the base of the cliff, and all four ladders were required to reach the uppermost rooms. Mearns noted that the juniper timbers supporting them still showed the bite of stone axes, and handprints remained on the plastered walls.

Neither before Mearns nor since have the relics of Montezuma Castle been sifted so thoroughly. Some distinguished turn-of-the-century archeologists, however, visited the Valley. Jesse Walter Fewkes of the Smithsonian's Bureau of American Ethnology, who had done excavation and stabilization at Mesa Verde and Casa Grande, came. So did Cosmos Mindeleff, also with the Bureau of American Ethnology. Although they surveyed and mapped extensively around the Verde, and their findings were important to later archeologists, they dug little.

Edgar Alexander Mearns
conducted the first archeological
excavation of Montezuma Castle
in the late 1800s and speculation
about prehistoric life here
continues today.

Interior of Montezuma Castle (left). Bone awl and twill-weave mat fragment (below). The room at right shows ceilings and walls fire-blackened from cooking fires.

Later, as with ruins almost everywhere, indiscriminate pot hunters, the "thieves of time," looted where they could. Their piracy, now inhibited by stringent statutes, has made interpretation of vanished cultures all the more difficult.

In 1916, though, the study of prehistory in northern Arizona got a boost. A patrician professor of zoology from the University of Pennsylvania, Harold Sellers Colton, moved to Flagstaff and quickly immersed himself in what would turn out to be nearly six decades of systematic study of the region's natural history and antiquity.

Among other things, he excavated a host of ancient sites in the piney highlands beneath the San Francisco Peaks and in the rolling high desert that drops eastward toward the Painted Desert. From their pottery types and other diagnostic differences, he noted that the people whose homes and possessions he uncovered were distinct from their neighboring contemporaries. Colton christened them the Sinagua.

Meanwhile, in the Valley to the south beneath the bulwark of the Mogollon Rim, the vestiges of the Sinagua had, since Mearns, remained mostly untouched by science. The Great Depression, ironically, changed that. As one way of treating an anemic national economy, federal funds were earmarked in the 1930s to hire the unemployed on public works projects. Some of that money financed excavations at Montezuma Castle and Tuzigoot.

At the urging of the Yavapai Chamber of Commerce in Prescott, the head of the University of Arizona anthropology department, Dr. Byron Cummings, and two of his graduate students surveyed the Valley for a large ruin to excavate. They finally chose one across the Verde River from the copper-smelting town of Clarkdale. To an untrained eye, the location would have seemed no more than a jumble of stones, cloaked by the dust of five centuries. The stones, in fact, were Sinagua walls.

Backing for the project came from the Federal Civil Works Administration, or CWA, and the students, Louis Caywood and Edward Spicer, hired 48 shovel-and-broomhands from among the local jobless. Together, they worked from the end of October of 1933 through the following May, excavating and partially restoring the village.

When they began, the place was without a name, until they adopted one proposed by an Apache workman: Tuzigoot, or "Crooked Water," after nearby Pecks Lake. Until the construction of a visitor center before Tuzigoot became a national monument in 1939, the artifacts they screened were displayed in an old store in Clarkdale which was owned by the United Verde Mining Company.

Tuzigoot had been suggested to Caywood and Spicer by a former classmate at the university, Earl Jackson, and a month after the Tuzigoot "dig" began, Jackson launched a CWA-supported excavation of his own at Montezuma Castle. Jackson almost literally grew up around the Castle, and his father, Martin, was its first custodian, at $10 a month. The family had homesteaded a mile away in 1917, eleven years after the area was made a national monument; Earl was seven then, and thirteen when he helped repair the Castle's weathered facade.

By the depression, Park Service officials decided Montezuma Castle was too fragile for excavation and that, Mearns probably had denuded it of artifacts. An alternative was to shovel out the contemporaneous Castle A, 100 yards down the same cliff face. Castle A

A coil weave basket made of split cottonwood twigs and Spanish bayonet.

had been twice the size of the four-story Montezuma Castle; it encompassed five floors, the lowest of them ten feet above the present creek terrace, and at least two dozen rooms. Some time after they were vacated, the cliff dwellings burned and crashed down the slope below.

This was "the crumbled mass" through which Jackson, laboratory technician Sallie Pierce Van Valkenburgh (another University of Arizona classmate) and 10 part-time workmen delved from mid-December 1933 until the following April.

As with Caywood and Spicer at Tuzigoot, they gingerly removed a lode of artifacts, each a testament to Sinagua life. Some very young archeologists had met some very old Indians.

INTO THE VALLEY

Precisely who the first Valley residents were and exactly from where they materialized may always be shadowed by the dimness of the distant past. Other wanderers may have preceded them, only to have whatever clues were left in their wake buried by centuries of water-washed soil. We do know that stalkers of game and foragers for wild plants trekked into the Valley at least 2,000 and perhaps as long as 8,000 years ago, most likely as scant, ragged groups of related families. Archeologists identify them by their implements.

Why they waited so long baffles researchers because people of the Clovis Culture had hunted along other southwestern streams several millenia earlier, when the Verde already offered fertile sanctuary. These later adventurers, when they did come, must have eked a living

15

The excavation of Tuzigoot by Louis Caywood and Edward Spicer began in the fall of 1933. The first artifacts that it yielded were displayed at the local high school. A Sinaguan stone-bead and turquoise necklace. This five foot strand was found at Tuzigoot (below).

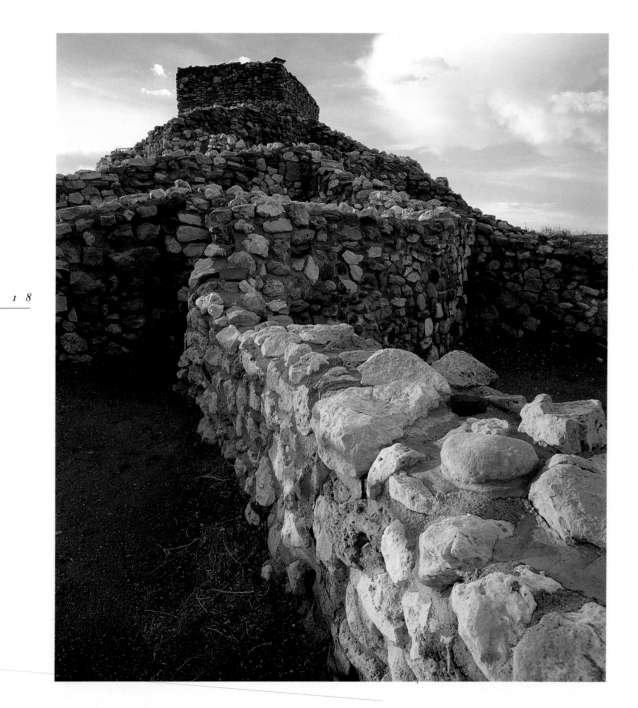

Tuzigoot (far left). Manos, or hand grinding stones, and metates, were used by the Sinaguan Indians to grind corn and other seeds (left). Room blocks at Tuzigoot (right).

in much the same nomadic manner as the Apache and Yavapai did when the Spaniards stumbled upon them. They wandered a wide area, timing their travels with the seasonal emergence of the flora.

Most of the unique projectile points of the initial Valley people were chipped from rocks not available nearby; thus one can assume they were Archaic Indians from elsewhere. Such points together with grinding stones (manos and metates) have turned up mainly along the branches of Oak Creek.

Whether they were ancestors of the Sinagua is uncertain. Some archeologists contend that the Sinagua were part of a larger, shifting, aggregation they call the Hakataya. Be that as it may, at some point, wanderers settled in dispersed, mainly underground rectangular dwellings called "pithouses." The rounded-end structures were shallow; holes in the floor provided places for fires and for storage. Since they were small, they must have been meant for single families.

Beyond their hardware and the traces of their pithouses, little has been learned about these homesteaders or the fragile lifestyle they pursued for at least 2,000 years. The Valley was clearly Sinagua by about A.D. 600-700, contact and commerce with other areas soon followed. The consequences of this interchange proved to be profound. Pottery was imported from the Kayenta Anasazi, who tilled the high desert along the Little Colorado River and elsewhere to the north, and from the Hohokam, the irrigators of central and southern Arizona.

At about the same time, and long after it took root in numerous, less hospitable parts of the Southwest, agriculture appeared in the Valley. Hunting and gathering perhaps had provided an adequate diet anyway. But while the Sinagua still foraged for wild edibles, they started, like the Anasazi and Hohokam, to grow corn, beans and squash. Increasing population may have been one reason.

Evidence for this transition lies in the evolution of millstones. To grind seeds requires a circular motion, so the early metates were round. Now, the metates were trough-shaped to facilitate the crushing of corn.

The Sinagua almost certainly learned to farm from the Hohokam. Hohokam traders ventured north along the Verde River and through the passageway created by the primal lakes, to barter for salt, copper and argillite, a red, clayey stone prized for ornamentation. Gradually, beguiled by the basin's fertility, many of them returned with their families to stay.

Archeologists still are uncertain of the relative size of the Hohokam exodus, or the extent to which it affected the Sinagua. But some think that between A.D. 700 and 800, the Hohokam began building their own architecturally unique pithouses. Some of the new residents settled among the Sinagua, some alongside them, and others in decidedly Hohokam neighborhoods. The sophistication of the southerns, more and more, influenced the established communities.

Dry farming developed, a technique for controlling moisture brought by the infrequent rains. Check dams were built to direct water onto terraced fields bordered with stone. Dry farming took place both in the lowlands and on the sunlit, more moist mesa tops.

Projects of such magnitude and, even more, the building and maintenance of irrigation systems dictated a communal cooperation beyond the experience of nomads. In turn, the teamwork kindled social cohesion and cultural

Rocky Mountain irises.

2 0

advancement, fomenting the rise of crafts-workers. In the Valley, Sinagua pottery was produced for the first time. It was rudimentary, to be sure, plain in color and without decorations, not unlike Hohokam ceramics of the time.

We know that the population and cultural changes burgeoned in this period. These can be measured in retrospect by the dimensions of dwellings. Pithouses were roomier and dug deeper, and they began to be round rather than rectangular. Moreover, the people began to occupy two- and three-room pueblos, many of them concentrated in the riverbottom where agriculture would have been most fruitful. A handful of the pithouses, like those still seen near Montezuma Well, were unusually large, suggesting that they were community centers or even regional hubs of commerce or religion.

One can envision the Hohokam as a kind of merchant class. Not the least intriguing of the concepts they brought, however, were two features infrequently found north of the Salt River: stylized platform mounds and ball courts. Archeologists once thought the mounds were merely huge trash heaps but have concluded they were conceived specifically for ceremonial use.

Eight of the ball courts have been unearthed in the Valley. Researchers conjecture they may have been patterned after similar courts in Mexico, where they were utilized for ritualized games.

By around A.D. 1000, then, the southern Sinagua country had been transformed from a backwater of hunters and gatherers into a busy domain of agriculture and trade. Nonetheless, the greatest growth and the pinnacle of progress were yet to come.

A LIMESTONE OASIS

Other than scatters of olive-drab creosote bushes, little colors the rolling, dun landscape of the Upper Sonoran Desert grassland. Surmounting a small hill six miles up Beaver Creek from Montezuma Castle, however, one can look to the east and down at a striking contrast to this arid land. Fields green with crops evoke what life was like here eight centuries or so ago, with irrigated Indian gardens of cotton, corn, squash and beans.

Atop the rise, the reason abruptly becomes evident. A blue-green pool peers up from a deep circular cup 470 feet across, constructed by Nature from the bottom up. Below, from a vent at the base of the hill, a million and a half gallons of water a day pours out toward the creek.

Scientists theorize that the cup was millions of years in the making. Underground water percolating upward formed a "springmound," a bulge of magnesium and calcium carbonate. Lens-shaped salt layers beneath the mound dissolved, creating caverns, until at last the weight of the layers of calcium carbonate, or travertine, collapsed downward through the salt lenses, and Montezuma Well yawned open.

Warm artesian springs replenish its contents, as much as 55 feet deep and a constant 70 feet below the sink's rim. Typical of subterranean water, the "well" is so charged with carbon dioxide that water fleas and microscopic rotifers, common in most ponds, are unable to survive. Nor can fish, which cannot breathe in high concentrations of carbon dioxide.

Other aquatic creatures abound, nonetheless. Muskrats and turtles paddle about. In winter, black-headed Canada geese, green-winged teals and mallards, with their chestnut breasts, alight. And the murky water obscures a nocturnal universe of smaller, less obvious creatures, at least six of them species that exist nowhere else on Earth. Isolation and the year-around consistency of water temperature and water chemistry—nutrients—presaged their adaptation to this place and time.

Hundreds of thousands of tiny shrimplike crustaceans rise at nightfall to feed at the open surface on algae and are fed upon themselves by swimming leeches and twiglike water scorpions. All of these, the crustaceans, the algae, the leeches and water scorpions, are peculiar to the Well.

No other freshwater shrimplike crustaceans are known to filter feed, as these do. They eat by combing algae cells through hairlike appendages just below their mouths. The water scorpions also are unlike any others. Most water scorpions perch among tangles of pond weeds, like a spider awaiting a careless insect, and grasp passing prey with their forelegs. This furtiveness is perhaps a defense against predatory fish. Here, where there are no fish, the water scorpions lurk close to shore half submerged among the weeds during the day, then at night swim slowly and awkwardly out in search of crustaceans.

The crustaceans are further unusual, in that most of their relatives rarely squirm far from protective weeds. Biologists are beguiled by what they think is an aquatic environment dissimilar to any other in the world.

But the magnet for ancient agriculturists was the more than 1,000 gallons of water pouring each minute from beneath the sink. Fifty yards of limestone separate an inlet within the pond and the outlet into the creek; the water flows through the stone in seven minutes.

2   1

Montezuma Well (left).
Prehistoric stone pick axes like
this were probably used to
construct the irrigation canals at
Montezuma Well (below). The
Sinagua diverted water from
Montezuma Well to irrigate their
fields (right).

In the fourteenth century, a
farming community of about
150–200 people inhabited the area
around Montezuma Well (left).

The ruins of several small
settlements are tucked into the
walls surrounding the Well
(above).

Around the outlet, the 75-degree water sustains a miniature jungle of watercress and maidenhair fern. Penstemon and columbine, in late spring, brush the thicket with scarlet reds and golden yellows.

With rough stone tools, the first farmers engineered a mile-long irrigation ditch, an average of three feet deep, and diverted the outlet water into it. About 60 acres of land were watered this way. About 600 pounds of dissolved lime float from the Well every day. That has preserved and coated the ditch with thick, waterproofing travertine that impedes seepage and evaporation and resists erosion.

Both the Hohokam and the Sinagua planted the lowlands around Montezuma Well. How early irrigation began is unclear, although the population apparently peaked during the fourteenth century with a farming community of between 150 and 200 people.

Architecture varied with time, from the partly underground pithouses of the earliest Hohokam to later, more complex Sinagua pueblos. The outline of a Hohokam pithouse can be seen near the Well. While the walls of poles, brush and mud long ago crumbled, the large size of the hard-packed floor hint at a town hall or ritualistic center.

Several small settlements, likely Sinagua, were tucked into the wall of the Well, one of them near the water level. Others, also built of stone, crowded the rim. A three-story complex of perhaps 55 rooms stood sentinel beside the only trails down into the sink. The lower floors may have been solidly walled, with ladders for roof-top entrance.

Compared with prehistoric peoples over most of the Southwest, these farmers and their relatives at Tuzigoot and Montezuma Castle, were blessed. Wild game and native plants were relatively plentiful, and most important, a ceaseless source of water was at hand.

Life was not an undiluted idyll, though, for they may have had enemies, unknown now, whose presence could account for the location of the large pueblo at the trailhead. There is evidence for a bizarre attack, or more, on one resident.

When the remains of a woman, who died between 30 and 35 years of age, were studied late in the 1930s, it was found that three obsidian arrowheads had pierced her skull. She seemed to have survived two of them long enough for the bone to heal over the projectiles, still embedded in her head. She may have succumbed to the third, or else to formidable headaches.

*T*HE CORRIDOR: SEEDS OF CHANGE

A time of terror exploded in about A.D. 1064 upon the Sinagua along the eastern slopes of the San Francisco Peaks. The Earth shuddered and ruptured, spewing out sulphuric fumes and black cinders that darkened the days. Lava tumbled down a fiery, five-mile flow. The eruptive debut of Sunset Crater was remaking the face of northern Arizona and casting the fate of the tribesmen of the entire region.

Amply warned, by the smoke and sounds, the nearby Indians escaped the volcanic wrath with most of their possessions; some even saved the poles that supported their roofs. Many of them fled south into the Verde Valley.

The volcano flared intermittently, if less forcefully than at first, for almost two centuries, hurling half a billion tons of ash across 800 square miles. (John Wesley Powell, the one-armed explorer of the Grand Canyon, bestowed its name in 1885, because the crimson cone reminded him of an endless sunset).

Much later, bands of the Sinagua returned to the Sunset Crater area, joined by other people from other directions. Cinders and volcanic ash, they discovered to their delight, made a moisture-retaining mulch that enabled them to grow crops in places previously too dry.

Harold Colton was convinced that this phenomenon triggered a "prehistoric land rush." Indeed, later experiments with corn confirmed that the cinders promote germination and plant height. Still, other scholars argue that the post-eruption population influx, while large, was not abnormal for that era of shifting-sands migrations, and that favorable climate played as critical a part as the cinders in enhancing agriculture. From year to year, the annual growth rings in certain trees fluctuate in width as a consequence of precipitation and temperatures. These southwestern tree-ring records show the years between 1050 and 1130 were extraordinarily wet and warm.

The Hohokam influence around modern Camp Verde crested at about the time of the eruption. Now, the masonry construction and ceramic types of the north became prevalent (although pueblos and pithouses often were erected side by side), and bartering grew with the northern Anasazi. Eventually, the mark of the Hohokam, once so pervasive along the Verde, all but disappeared, along with such tell-tale traits of the southerners as ball courts and the burial of cremated human remains in pottery vessels.

Tribal divisions were not always marked. Besides the sharing of resources and technology, intermarriage increased, and from this more homogenous group the founders of more advanced villages were to stem.

Between 1130 and 1300, dwellings shrank in size, and larger communal rooms mushroomed, suggesting a stable social structure. This was the so-called Honanki Phase, after a then-typical village in the red rock country near Sedona. Honanki, according to the tree-ring researchers, was built in approximately 1271.

Farmers today would find the gravel-strewn canyon bottom thickets forbidding. Yet the slender side canyons were dotted by houses with smoke-blackened ceilings and storage bins containing corn cobs. In a period of above-normal rainfall and snowfall, additional springs and seeps probably trickled in the rocky terrain.

Farming flourished, too, along the uplands overlooking the Valley. Because cold night air wafting down from the mountains collects in lower elevations, the warmer mesa tops are endowed with longer growing seasons than the Valley floor.

New kinds of communities came into being late in this phase: buildings knotted at the summit of hills or at the entrance to canyons. Often they were backed against cliff faces, with walled fronts. Were these fortifications? Archeologists do not concur. Without indications of any real warfare, some scientists have decided that population growth must have strained the food supply, and thus "forts" were built to guard farmlands.

Not so, some of their colleagues respond. The "forts," they say, sprouted along transportation trails and were rife with imported pottery; hence they must have served some commercial purpose at a time of intensified trade.

Whatever the explanation, these specialized structures spread, and it was then, about a millineum ago, that the earlier rooms went up at Tuzigoot and Montezuma Castle.

HIGH-RISES AND HILLTOP FORTS

From the testimony of middens and burials, vignettes emerge of the lifestyle, the artistry and even the physical appearance of the Sinagua. But the masonry of their final few centuries here evidence the blossoming of their culture and is their most indelible contribution.

Unequalled now simply because they remain, the settlements that survive were not extraordinary at the time. Cliff houses similar to Montezuma Castle crowded the canyons, and though most were smaller, the Valley was strewn with towns like hill-top Tuzigoot.

Both villages began some time before the year A.D. 1000 with a few rooms and, like the architecture that sets them apart, took shape slowly. At Tuzigoot, rounded river boulders, often darkly volcanic, and other stone was used to construct the first rooms. This distinguished them from the later rooms, built of soft limestone, white and sometimes pinkish, quarried from the old lake beds. Because the limestone was rough and irregular, structurally stable walls did not always come about. They were massive, all the same. Even after excavation, some still stood 12 feet high.

This perch, lording loftily over miles of the Valley, perhaps was chosen for fortification, or perhaps for totally unrelated reasons. Possibly its builders liked the view.

Tuzigoot, at one point, stretched for 500 feet along the ridge, 120 feet above the Verde River. Typical of southwestern ruins, rooms often were deserted and, later, new rooms stacked over them. One room was emptied so early that eventually it was inundated by 11 feet of trash; to the archeologists, that meant several centuries.

Sometime between 1000 and 1200, the number of residents declined, then increased again. But when complete abandonment came about 1425, as it also did at Montezuma Castle, 77 ground-floor rooms were inhabited, several of them with second and perhaps third stories. Caywood and Spicer calculated a peak population of 450 people, although archeologists now think there were only about 225.

Most of the Tuzigoot homes covered about 18 by 12 feet, larger than the 100-square-foot average of those in the more crowded confines at Montezuma Castle. Construction challenges at Montezuma Castle proved more formidable, as building materials had to be carried up the cliff the same way the people got into their homes, by ladders. Not surprisingly, the limestone used was smaller than that at Tuzigoot, usually no larger than two bricks.

Probably the ladders were single logs with notches incised into them for footholds, or were made by tying rungs across upright

Small doorways at Montezuma

Castle caused speculation among

early pioneers that the ancient

inhabitants were midgets.

T-shaped doorways are common

in Montezuma Castle but

archeologists still debate their

purpose.

The Black Hills (left). Looking across Verde Valley toward the red rocks of Sedona (right).

poles. Ropes no doubt helped in hoisting into place the sycamore logs installed as roof beams. Notching the foot-thick beams with stone axes could not have been easy.

As the stones were fitted together, they were mortared, as at Tuzigoot, with clay mud. Plaster also veneered the interior of the foot-thick walls, curved to conform to the cave's contours. Unlike Tuzigoot, where almost every room had a fire pit, cooking at Montezuma Castle primarily was done outdoors.

Sinagua doors were so small that many pioneers (those who did not believe in giants) insisted the aboriginals must have been midgets. Actually, the men averaged five feet, four inches in height. Though only scarcely shorter, the Sinagua had longer heads and broader noses than most modern Americans. As for the small doors, the explanations could include security and keeping out winter cold and summer heat.

Intertwined poles and twigs, smeared with mud, roofed the Castle. It was a four-story complex, not counting two "basement" storage caves, of 17 rooms and occupied by 45 to 50 people. But these buildings housed the dead as well as the living.

Traditional Navajo shun homes where anyone has died. No such fear of ghosts haunted the Sinagua and, in contrast to the Hohokam, who usually cremated their deceased, the Sinagua interred their corpses closeby. Babies were buried in the floors of their parents' houses, a custom carried on by the Hopi well into historic time.

Virtually every room at Tuzigoot and Castle A contained baby bones, often swaddled in twilled matting. One room, at the former, held four infants who had died at different times. Usually the skeleton of one child would simply be moved aside to make way for another, and the sandstone-slab cover then replaced. Infant deaths were rampant among the Sinagua, as they still are among many less technologically advanced peoples.

Life generally was brief. Few adults lived beyond age 40, and when they died, their faces occasionally were stained green and blue and their heads were swathed with rush matting. Cotton burial robes sometimes clothed them.

Corn, beans and squash were the major food crops. Corn, husbanded by hybridization from the wild grasses that were its ancestors, had spread into the Southwest from Mexico generations earlier. Beans followed shortly, tamed in roughly the same era and area. Whether this was by chance or through some strange Indian insight, it was fortunate. Corn lacks an essential amino acid—lysine—in which beans are rich.

Prehistoric growers gardened along Beaver Creek with the overflow from Montezuma Well. With water diverted from the Verde River, the Tuzigoot families farmed the flatlands to the east and west of their ridge; the fields to the west now are obscured by 60 feet of tailings from the Clarkdale smelter.

Even when their fields yielded adequate food, however, the people of the Valley continued to supplement their fare with wild plants. Southwestern tribes still, to some degree, utilize the native flora, and that allows us to guess which plants were used prehistorically. Lamb's quarter, a weed with arrow-shaped leaves, was boiled with saltbush leaves and roasted cholla buds to serve as a sort of vegetable stew.

Agaves, or century plants, were pit-baked and the leaves then removed, leaving a slimy but sweet hunk about the size of a cauliflower.

An eagle-shaped pendant found in a burial at Castle A at Montezuma Castle.

The purposes to which plants were put were vast: chewing gum from milkweed and white brittlebush, and a rocklike candy from ocotillo-blossom nectar. Seeds from pigweed (or amaranth) were winnowed and saved for winter meals. Even now, an invigorating citrine drink is stirred from sumac—the squawbush or lemonade berry.

Shrubs and herbs heal as well as furnishing food. Hundreds of them still provide the Navajo and Hopi with medicinals, although no more than a few may be known to any one herbalist.

Pounded on a rock or chewed into a pulp, four-wing saltbush is said to ease the stings of ants and bees, while pinyon pitch, rubbed on sores, serves as a linament. Other medicinal plants are widespread, among them the cliff-fendlerbush, whose pink-tinged white flowers exude a fragrance of oranges, and the jimson weed. The fendlerbush is thought to act as an aphrodisiac for men and has been used as a cathartic. The poisonous jimsonweed, also white-flowered, may be applied as a poultice for cuts and sprains.

A handful of plants fill a variety of purposes, none of them more than the utilitarian *Yucca baccata*, or Spanish dagger. Its fat, bananalike fruits are a favored food. A lather formed from the roots is used as soap, as well as to heal heartburn, and the wide, stiff leaves, pulverized and added to water, are an antidote to vomiting.

And so, despite her demands, Nature somehow provided, and the tides of the generations flowed and ebbed. In these places so very old themselves, aged people once rested and died, and yet children played. There was time for toys—such as miniature pots—and for games of some sort with doughnut-shaped stone rings.

From the sweeping vista of the Valley on the Tuzigoot ridge and along Beaver Creek, shaded by sycamores and netleaf hackberries and musical with the calls of Gambel's quails, life could not have been all unpleasant.

CRAFTSMEN AND TRADERS

Grave offerings furnish archeologists with economic indicators of the life and times of the Sinagua and their appreciation for the aesthetic. Wealth was to be had, albeit wealth distributed unevenly.

Mostly the dead were interred with no earthly goods, or no more perhaps than a few simple, undecorated red bowls. But there were exceptions. A bracelet of tiny turquoise beads, carefully carved to represent birds, was found with an infant's remains at Tuzigoot, and the resting places of a few residents there, probably the most prosperous or priestly, literally were treasure troves.

Caywood and Spicer, in their first week of excavation, unearthed what they called "the priest burial;" a man had been laid out in a prepared stone cist and covered with thin red sandstone slabs. Woven matting wreathed his upper body and head, and a full collection of ceramics made up the more modest part of his possessions.

Around his neck looped a twelve-and-a-half-foot necklace fashioned from 3,295 small beads of black and red stone and white shell. Three diminutive mosaic-frog ear pendants, of turquoise inlaid in seashells, dangled from the neckpiece. The deceased also wore 13 glycimeris shell bracelets and a wrist ornament, five feet long, of stone beads. A minute mask of olivella shell beads and other shell fragments apparently was sewn onto a garment that had since disintegrated.

Except for one more, that of a man left with a painted basket and a large, though lesser, array of jewelry, most of the 408 Tuzigoot tombs that were opened were unimpressive. The archeologists were awed, all the same, with what they observed on the hill beside the Verde. "Almost every article of jewelry," they wrote, "tells a story of infinite skill, infinite patience, a passionate love of ornament and a very fine and true taste for beauty."

Ornaments from the burials in Castle A at Montezuma Castle were similar though, inexplicably, generally less lavish. One outstanding piece was an eagle-shaped shell pendant set with a miniature bird of 85 pieces of turquoise. A gum glued the turquoise in place, probably the standard Sinagua adhesive, the shellaclike lac that insects secrete on plants.

Which of all this jewelry was crafted locally and which was obtained through trade is difficult to say. Some must have originated with both sources, although trade was a key ingredient of pre-European existence in North America. Without money, life would have been one long swap meet.

In exchange for salt, copper, cotton and argillite, the Sinagua received pottery from both north and south and marine shells from the Gulf of California. The shells were brought by the Hohokam, whose arduous journeys to gather them may have been as much religious pilgrimages, to beseech the ocean for rain, as they were business trips.

The stock of the traveling salesmen could

have been considerable in scope: medicinal and edible herbs possibly, and gewgaws of various kinds. A parrot that had to have been imported from Mexico was buried with care in a stone-lined pit beneath a Tuzigoot floor. At Montezuma Castle, Edgar Mearns came upon a heavy block of red catlinite, or pipestone, and tiny fetishes formed from it. Catlinite can be quarried only along the Upper Missouri River. Many archeologists today believe that the stone was argillite of a more local origin rather than catlinite.

Artifacts relate much about the subsistence of people long gone, and about their creativity. For example, no tool may be too mundane to decorate; workman at Tuzigoot incised likenesses of birds on the heads of bone awls or hairpins. Paint palettes turned up at Montezuma Castle, as well as miniature pottery, clay human effigies, decorated prayer sticks and doughnut-shaped stone disks presumably used for games. A section of cane could have held smoking tobacco.

The majority of the items were more workaday, however, such as stone axes and picks, sandals plaited from yucca leaves, yucca fiber skirts, bark whorls for spinning cotton and dyed cotton fabric.

Oddities like these and the glamorous jewelry excite the imagination and enrich museums, but the archeologists' true stock-in-trade, not so spectacular, is pottery fragments. Potsherds are the time pieces of archeology. Because different ceramics developed in different settings during specific times, times that often

can be correlated with precise tree-ring dates, they allow one to fit prehistoric events into the modern calendar.

The Sinagua were not renowned for their pottery. They made plain, unadorned red and coarse brown wares—Tuzigoot Red and Verde Brown—that instead of becoming more artful over the centuries actually grew more crude. Perhaps it was easier to trade for pots manufactured elsewhere.

If sherds are the grails of archeologists, their Camelots are trash heaps. Fortunately, the residents at Tuzigoot disposed of their broken pots and other discards simply by throwing them down the west slope of the hill. The refuse accumulated generation after generation.

The excavators dug an 11-foot-deep trench across the slope, exposing the entire span of the village's occupancy. From the layers of pottery, the oldest at the bottom of the trench, the most recent at the top, they then could decipher the Sinagua story the same way geologists read the Earth's history from strata of stone.

Painstakingly trowelling out the thousands of broken bits, the scientists catalogued separately each layer of the dump. Most of the ceramic scraps were from the plain pottery produced in the Valley. Over the entire era, though, exotic material appeared, such as black-on-red bowls and multicolored Anasazi pots, geometrically painted, from the north on what now is the Navajo Reservation.

At the depths of the debris, the predominant pottery was one called Kana-a Black-on-white. Pottery types are named for their place of origin, and Kana-a is a small stream near Flagstaff. And at the top was a proliferation of Jeddito Black-on-yellow sherds from north of Winslow. Jeddito (Navajo for antelope) Black-on-yellow was the most common pottery at

both Tuzigoot and Montezuma Castle, not surprising since it came when they were at their most populous.

Here, then, were the brackets within which the cities of the Sinagua could be dated. Kana-a Black-on-white was not made before about A.D. 950, and Jeddito Black-on-yellow only until around 1400.

*A*BANDONMENT: THE ABIDING RIDDLES
By about A.D. 1425, the settlements were ghost towns. At the Spaniards' entrada, not much more than a century later, eddies of desert dust had long ago erased the footprints at Tuzigoot, and Montezuma Castle was quiet save for the songs of birds and the soft ripples of Beaver Creek. The Valley was virtually as bereft of residents as it had been 600 years before.

Strangely, their stone cities had been at once the apex of attainment for the Sinagua and a portent of their end as an identifiably different people. The mystery of their departure defies solution, since every explanation proposed simply provokes more questions.

To compound the enigma, the phenomenon was widespread. All the ancient Southwest's great centers of culture were abandoned within a few centuries of one another. Tuzigoot and Montezuma Castle, the Anasazi's Mesa Verde and Chaco Canyon, and the Hohokam's Casa Grande and Snaketown: all were deserted in what U.S. Forest Service archeologist Peter Pilles calls their "golden age."

RUINS ALONG THE RIVER

Sinagua pottery is characterized by unadorned red and brown wares. This type of bowl is referred to by archeologists as "Tuzigoot red."

That more artifacts were not left behind hints at a somewhat leisurely leave-taking at Tuzigoot and Montezuma Castle. Had the inhabitants been routed by invaders, there should have been signs of enemy armaments; there were none.

Water-logging of irrigated farms and the break-up of trade networks have been evoked as explanations, as had disease. Sanitary conditions certainly could have festered as the once dispersed aboriginals crowded into villages. (A small visitor to Montezuma Castle once asked his mother: "Where did they go the bathroom?" She thought a moment and then replied: "I don't know. Maybe that's why they moved.")

Skeletal evidence shows that many children died of anemia, an effect of deficient diet. Did Sinagua society fail because the people were unable to reproduce in sufficient numbers? The most compelling argument for abandonment is for a change in climate to dryer conditions. Tree-ring chronologies reveal that drought devastated the whole region from 1276 to 1299. While that would have doomed the dry-farmed fields of the Anasazi, the usually well-watered Verde Valley must have remained a comparative haven. Why, then, was it left behind?

One could conclude there was no single reason, but a combination of causes. Whatever they were, the dislocations raise the spectre of where the survivors went, and who their descendants are. Some of the Anasazi surely joined the Hopi (the "Peaceful People") while others migrated to the Rio Grande and were assimilated there by the ancestors of the present-day Pueblo Indians. Archeologists cannot agree on the fate of the Hohokam, but the trail of the Sinagua seems a little clearer. A few may have joined the nomadic Yavapai, who were filtering in from the west when the Sinagua settlements were being vacated and who still were in the Valley when the Spaniards encountered them. Nonetheless, scholars believe very few did.

Many more Sinagua almost indisputably wended their way north to be integrated among the ancestral Hopi villages of Homolovi near Winslow and Nuvakwewtaqa close by in Chavez Pass. The oral histories related by older Hopi, particularly members of the Water Clan, speak of tribal roots in cliff dwellings to the south. And, it is told, the Spaniards were led by the Hopi along an old trail linking the Hopi mesas through Chavez Pass and down Beaver Creek with the Verde Valley. Sinagua blood may course through the people of the mesas.

Solutions to these riddles are not beyond hope. Archeologists continue to fit pieces of the puzzle together, using scientific tools and techniques beyond the boldest ambitions of the 1930s. Archeomagnetic dating and radiocarbon dating, as examples, had not been imagined then.

Already, however, Tuzigoot and Montezuma Castle may have a lesson to impart. Their builders attained an impressive degree of artistry and cultural cohesion in a period when simple survival demanded ingenuity. The Sinagua dominated their environment for more centuries than the United States has lasted, and yet no one knows with certainty what became of them. The lesson, then, is that no matter how vibrant a society seems to be at a given time, Nature or social conflict still can overrule.

3 5

FORT VERDE

Fort Verde, first garrisoned by a handful of hapless volunteers in 1865, was abondoned almost as ingloriously in 1891. In between, however, the post provided a crucial link in the chain of bases established to subdue the Indians. It was there on the porch of the commanding officer's quarters, in 1873, that Cha-lipun surrendered some 2,300 of his Apaches to General George Crook, ending most of the native resistance in northern Arizona.

Responding to complaints of Indian attacks from the pioneering white farmers, 20 volunteers were sent into the Valley from Prescott in 1865. En route, their wagon was wrecked, then set upon and burned by the enemy. The soldiers arrived afoot and virtually without supplies. For years, troops at the make-shift camp of tents were beleaguered by malaria, underpaid (or paid not at all) and sometimes had to make their own shoes. At least once, upon capturing a band of Indians, they found the Indians had been eating better than they.

Conditions improved once regular Army troops arrived in 1866 and for most of its remaining history, two companies each of cavalry and infantry were stationed at Verde. The final post, constructed in 1871-73, consisted of 20 buildings blanking a parade ground; four of those structures and parts of others remain as part of the Fort Verde State Historic Park.

After his foes were subjugated, the compassionate Crook proposed, and the government set aside, 800 acres in the Valley as a reservation for them. The idea was self sufficiency and, indeed, the vanquished people soon were irrigating 56 acres. But their anglo neighbors coveted that land, and in 1875 the Indians were exiled to the San Carlos Reservation in eastern Arizona. Almost 1,500 of them were forced to march for 10 days in the February cold; about 100 froze to death or succumbed to starvation.

Officers' quarters
at Fort Verde State Park.

JEROME

If Jerome indeed is a "ghost town," as its few hundred residents (down from 15,000 in 1929) like to say, it must be one of the busiest. Although the town always has perched precariously high on the brow of Mingus Mountain in the Black Hills, its fortunes soared and plummeted with the price of copper.

Claims on the copper deposits first were staked in 1876 by local ranchers, but their enterprise showed little promise for several years until they obtained funds from a New Yorker, Eugene Jerome, the father of Winston Churchill's American mother. Still, the cost of shipping supplies into the remote location, and carrying copper out, proved prohibitive, and the operation was short lived.

Not until the Santa Fe Railroad reached Ashfork, 60 miles to the northwest, did mining become economically feasible. Coke for the smelter (later replaced by New Mexico coal) had to be shipped by steamer to San Francisco from Wales, transported by rail to Ashfork and finally hauled in wagons the final 60 miles. Despite that, the new owners were able to extract copper for as little as six cents a pound.

Fires repeatedly razed the ramshackle town, and water, even for drinking, always was a problem. In 1900, one entrepreneur transported water into town aboard his 200 burros; Pancho Villa later would become famous as a Mexican revolutionary.

The United Verde Mine was the most prolific copper producer in the Arizona Territory at that time. Twelve years thereafter, a second mine opened, the Little Daisy, and was acquired by mining magnate "Rawhide Jimmy" Douglas.

Douglas built a mansion that was a marvel then, and a tourist attraction (and state park) now. While the building was constructed of adobe bricks formed on the spot, it boasted marble-face bathrooms, a wine cellar, billiard room, steam heat and—astonishing in 1916—a central vacuum-cleaning system.

Copper mining ended in 1953, and today's Jerome primarily is a tourist attraction and haven for artisans. Its frame houses clinging precariously to the side of the mountain, the town features several good restaurants and offers an unparalleled view of the Verde Valley.

The hills below Jerome (above).

Jerome, Arizona (right).

3 8

SEDONA

Zane Grey, who lived there for awhile, was so inspired by "the deep abyss," that he wrote a book, The Call of the Canyon, *and visitors to Oak Creek Canyon have been equally awed ever since. Few places in the Southwest are so spectacular. From its source beneath the Mogollon rim, amid pines and spruce, the stream tumbles down almost 600 feet in less than a dozen miles, corseted by multihued cliffs, until it spills into the cactus country of Sedona.*

Newcomers to Sedona may sense an aura of deja vu, for scores of movies—and a procession of television commercials—have been filmed among the pastel spires and buttes, a setting that also has provided a pallette for generations of artists and photographers.

Founded in 1902 as a shopping center for surrounding ranches and fruit farms, Sedona took the name of the sister-in-law of the first postmaster. Until the 1950s, it was little more than that, a somnolent rural village. A lack of drinking water inhibited growth. But deep water wells were drilled, a modest boom began.

Although Sedona still studiously clings to much of its subdued, small-town ambience, galleries and art shows, chic shops and the homes of prosperous retirees have made the town a mecca for visitors.

The redrock country of Sedona
(left). The west fork of Oak Creek
Canyon (above).

―――――

Red Rock Crossing, Sedona (left).
Red Rock Secret Mountain
Wilderness, near Sedona (right).

FLAGSTAFF

A handful of frontiersmen first settled in 1876, beneath the San Francisco peaks, which soar to 12,670 feet, the highest point in Arizona. That July a band of scouts, sent ahead by colonists from Boston, camped there, and decided to celebrate the nation's centennial. They stripped the branches from a tall pine and tied an American flag to the top with rawhide strings. The "flagstaff" became a landmark for travelers, and the name stuck.

An inscription at the entrance to the Museum of Northern Arizona proclaims: "This museum displays ideas, not things." And his successors have successfully sought to preserve the philosophy of founder Harold Colton, that the museum should present concepts rather than simply a supermarket of faded pottery and old bones.

The ideas it displays illuminate the region's geology, biology and, most of all, the lives of Indians past and present. There is no better introduction to, nor refresher course on, the ethnology, natural history and prehistory of the Colorado Plateau, the Arizona highlands above the Mogollon Rim.

In order to display ideas, it is helpful to have some things, of course, and the museum presents a wondrous assortment: an ancient sloth skeleton, Navajo rugs, a dioramic cross-section of northern Arizona geology and a full-size reproduction of a Hopi kiva, or ceremonial chamber. The annual exhibitions and sales of Hopi and Navajo crafts in July and August are highlights.

Among other area attractions are an art museum, Northern Arizona University and the pioneer Riordan home. Flagstaff draws skiiers in the winter, and classical music lovers for a summer festival. Lowell Observatory, where the planet Pluto was discovered in 1930, opens to visitors at announced hours.

WALNUT CANYON

Just east of Flagstaff, Walnut Canyon wends its way for 20 miles, through the piney Colorado Plateau. In the deepest reach of this chasm, 400 feet below the slanting flatland, the Sinagua tucked cliff homes beneath protective overhangs; more than 400 rooms remain, averaging 80 square feet in size.

The residents, like their relatives at Montezuma Castle, jigsawed slabs of limestone for walls, mortaring and plastering them with clay and mud from a stream below. Almost all the dwellings contained firepits, and most had retaining walls on the canyon edge.

And, again, in common with the people of the Verde Valley, those of Walnut Canyon were potters, weavers, basketmakers and farmers who tended corn, beans and squash, mostly planted on the Canyon's rim. Although they put up small dams to retain water, they did not irrigate, depending instead on rainfall (the annual average precipitation now is about 20 inches) to water their crops. Cotton, which cannot grow at this 7,000-foot elevation, had to be obtained by barter.

To supplement what they planted, wild game would have been plentiful. There must have been fish in a creek, probably permanent, that gushed down the canyon until the early 1900s when Flagstaff, already growing and needing more water, dammed it upstream.

From what we know of other Indians, past and present, one can assume they used the utilitarian yucca and picked wild potatoes, grapes, blueberries and elder, all at hand. Barberry, a bush that resembles holly, furnished wood for weaving implements and arrowshafts, as well as a bright yellow dye.

Because many prehistoric artifacts were vandalized before Walnut Canyon was made a national monument in 1915, scientists can simply speculate about many aspects of the ancient life here. Based on the number and sizes of the rooms, archeologists estimate a peak population of around 500. From other evidence, they infer the dwellings were not built until after Sunset Crater erupted and were abandoned, as mysteriously as other Sinagua settlements, early in the 1200s.

Coiled basket sealed with pine pitch (far left). Courtesy of Wupatki National Monument. Ruins at Walnut Canyon.

SUNSET CRATER

"The contrast in the colors is so great," wrote explorer John Wesley Powell, "that on viewing the mountain from a distance the red cinders seem to be on fire. From this circumstance the cone has been named Sunset Peak." Although much of the cone is basaltic black the influence of iron particles has painted the rim red, giving it an almost golden glow.

Apollo 17 astronauts trained at the monument to learn about some of the geology they might encounter on the lunar surface, and an electrically driven moon cart called a "Grover" was tested there. But the most dramatic role proposed for the 1,000-foot-tall peak came much earlier, in 1928, when a movie maker proposed to recreate a volcanic eruption by blowing up the little mountain with dynamite. Harold Colton, the ubiquitous founder of the Museum of Northern Arizona, almost erupted himself. Incensed, he successfully pulled strings in Washington. Sunset Crater became a national monument in 1930, and thus was spared a short, and probably disastrous, film career.

The crater exploded intermittently for some two centuries, starting in about 1064, making the youngest of the more than 400 remnants of the 3,000-square-mile San Francisco volcanic field, a caldron of hadean fires and fumes that rumbled to life 1.8 million years ago.

Unlike the San Francisco Peaks, thrusting up to 12,633 feet eight miles to the west, Sunset is a cinder cone, formed from loose material fired up from a fissure in the ground. The San Francisco Peaks, like Mount St. Helens and Japan's Fujiyama, are composite volcanoes, built by lava flows and ash. (A third type, the gently rounded shield volcanoes that make such massive mountains as Mauna Loa in Hawaii, are constructed by successive, shallow streams of lava).

Less than 800 years later, this is a place more tranquil. Visitors explore the lava flows, witness the bizarre basaltic sculptures extruded from the peak and peer into a lava tube, or tunnel, punctuated with ice much of the year. Tuft-eared Abert's squirrels plunge among the pines; amid the chatter of crested Steller's jays. Lizards, adapted by darkening to the volcanic colors, dart across the crater.

WUPATKI

As the Sinagua region flowered following the final outbursts at Sunset Crater, its northern bastion became Wupatki, above the Little Colorado River. Eventually, the cosmopolitan center there included an open-air amphitheater and the most northerly Hohokam-style masonry ball court. The pueblos contained in excess of 2,000 structures at one time or another, some of them three stories high. Wupatki means "tall house" in Hopi.

Archeologists, once convinced this was a melting-pot city where different tribes settled together, now are less certain. Increasing evidence suggests, instead, that Wupatki was more a mercantile center and cultural crossroads, where goods changed hands and philosophies were discussed. One argument for this comes from re-analysis of the area's ceramics. If Anasazi potters, for instance, moved here from the north, their products would have to have been made from the local clay, filled with cinders. But the Anasazi pottery excavated at these sites held few if any cinders. Hence, the reasoning goes, it must have been imported by traders.

Geographically, Wupatki was in a prime location for such commerce, as its artifacts prove. Seashells and copper bells, as well as the remains of parrots and macaws, were unearthed. All of these are Hohokam trademarks.

The reign of the northern outpost was relatively brief, nonetheless, probably because the cinder mulch needed for farming soon was swept away. The winds of Wupatki are relentless. And so, by roughly the year 1190, all construction ceased. The people may have migrated southward into the Verde Valley, where the population still was mushrooming.

Navajo families had long lived in the area, and non-Navajo ranchers ran huge herds of livestock there, when it was made a national monument in 1924. Intruders arrived much earlier, however. Sheepherders moved into one room of Wupatki Ruins in the 1800s and installed a chimney in a corner, unaware that beneath them were the burials of six Sinagua children.

Sunset Crater, Sunset Crater National Monument (above).
Wukoki Ruins, Wupatki National Monument (right).

ACKNOWLEDGMENTS

Although the interpretations and any errors are his responsibility alone, the author is grateful for the consultation of geologist Larry Agenbroad, biologist Dean Blinn and archeologist Peter Pilles.

ADDITIONAL READING

Probably the best popular introduction to the region's archeology is *Those Who Came Before* (184 pp.) by Robert H. and Florence C. Lister, published in 1983 by the Southwest Parks and Monuments Association in Tucson.

For more detail, there is the lovely *The First American: A Story of North American Archaeology,* by C.W. Ceram (Harcourt Brace Jovanovich, Inc., 1971, 357 pp.).

John C. McGregor's *Southwestern Archaeology* (University of Illinois Press, 511 pp.), which first appeared in 1941 and has been updated in subsequent editions, is a standard text.

For readers with some scientific background and a thirst for more in-depth information, a number of technical reports may be found in libraries.

Dean W. Blinn and David B. Johnson describe one occupant of Montezuma Well in "Filter-feeding of Hyalella montezuma, an Unusual Behavior for a Freshwater Amphipod" in the *Journal of Freshwater Invertebrate Biology* (May 1982, v. 1 (2) pp. 48-52).

More has been written about the area's prehistory than its natural history, however. Two examples:

"Sunset Crater and the Sinagua: A New Interpretation," by Peter J. Pilles, Jr. in the book *Volcanic Activity and Human Ecology* (Payson Sheets and Donald Grayson, editors, Academic Press, 1979, pp. 459-485).

Tuzigoot: An Archaeological Overview, by Dana Hartman, Museum of Northern Arizona Research Paper 4 (1976, 80 pp.).

All these publications include extensive bibliographies that can lead the curious on to still more references.

The May 1981 and July 1983 issues of *Arizona Highways* magazine focus on the Verde Valley, as does a 1981 issue (Vol. 53, No. 1) of *Plateau,* a journal of the Museum of Northern Arizona in Flagstaff.

Sunset
Cook Book of
BREADS

By the Editors of Sunset Books and Sunset Magazine

Lane Publishing Co. • Menlo Park, California

When crumb and crust are perfect...

Few foods in today's wide-ranging gustatory repertoire are as simple, beautiful, and quietly delicious as freshly baked bread. Few are as satisfying to prepare.

Over the years, *Sunset* Magazine has tested, retested, and finally—when crumb and crust were perfect—published hundreds of bread recipes, the best of which are presented here. Many improve on traditional breads, updating Grandmother's methods to fit in with the busier schedules of today's world. Others explore new and tasty ways with whole grain flours. Still others adapt unusual breads from different cultures—some originally baked in outdoor ovens or under a campfire—so that the same crusty goodness can emerge from a modern kitchen.

Our very special thanks are due Lynne B. Morrall for her design ideas and sensitive handling of photographic situations.

Edited by: Susan Warton
Kandace Esplund Reeves

Photography: All photographs by Darrow M. Watt except page 70 by Norman A. Plate
Artwork: Patricia Kinley
Design and Calligraphy: Cynthia Hanson

Front cover: Bounty of breads includes, clockwise from lower left, Zuñi loaves and Arab Pocket Bread (both on page 47), Peda Bread I (page 44), Peda Bread II (page 45), Armenian Thin Bread (page 44), and Basque Sheepherder's Bread (page 42). Photograph by Darrow M. Watt.

Back cover: Super Simple Refrigerator Bread (page 11). Photograph by Darrow M. Watt.

Editor, Sunset Books: David E. Clark

Second Printing July 1978

Contents

A Basket of Yeast Breads

Clockwise from left: Finnish Farmer Bread (page 39), Basic White Bread (page 8), Party Bread Sticks (page 25), Onion Boards (page 23), and Pumpkin Pan Rolls (page 32).

People who have discovered the joy of baking yeast bread will tell you that it is one of the most satisfying experiences in the kitchen. For many bakers, kneading the soft dough is a lovely sensation, a sort of relaxing therapy. For others, the glorious moment comes with the first buttered bite of the fresh, warm loaf. For everyone, the yeasty aroma wafting from the oven as the bread bakes crowns the day with a sense of delicious achievement.

If you haven't yet tried your hand at the simple art of bread making, these next few pages are intended especially for you. (If you're already a baker, you may prefer to dive right into the array of recipes further along in the book.)

Yeast bread baking has the reputation of being chancy and difficult (as no doubt it was in past generations when people had to cultivate their own yeast and bake in wood-burning stoves). It's true that you do need to be careful at first. You have to protect the baby dough to get it started. But after that the bread almost makes itself.

For your first experience, it might be wise to try our Basic White Bread (page 8), following the step-by-step photos. After having baked a few loaves, you'll probably acquire a feel for such things as what constitutes "warm" and what is the right consistency of the dough at various stages.

What's In a Loaf — and Why

The staff of life is a supremely satisfying food. It is made of five basic ingredients which—through handiwork and something like magic—interplay to build a wholesome loaf.

Yeast is a microscopic plant; when activated by warm water it gives off bubbles of carbon dioxide that leaven dough (make it rise). Yeast is most commonly available in granular form—called "active dry yeast"—sold in packages of about 1 tablespoon each. It can be stored for about a year in a cool, dry place (the expiration date is printed on the package). Yeast is also sold in a compressed cake; the quantity is the same, but yeast in this form is much more perishable and must be refrigerated. It usually lasts up to 2 weeks. Test by crumbling it—if it crumbles readily, it is still good.

The recipes in this book call for the dry form of yeast because we have found it more widely available and more convenient for most bakers. Should you want to substitute compressed yeast, just be sure you dissolve it in lukewarm water (about 95°) rather than warm (about 110°) water.

Flour provides the structure and heartiness of bread. Many kinds of flour—even ground acorns—have been kneaded into loaves over the long history of bread making. A few interesting varieties are described under *Flour and Other Grain Products* on page 7.

For yeast breads, at least part of the flour must be wheat, which contains a curious protein called "gluten." When wheat flour is moistened and beaten, the gluten becomes very elastic, allowing the dough to stretch as the yeast leavens it and giving the loaf enough strength to keep its shape when baked. Rye flour is also glutenous, though less so than wheat, which is why it is usually combined with whole wheat or all-purpose flour.

The amount of flour needed in any recipe or on any given day will vary according to minute factors of moisture in the flour, as well as temperature and humidity of the air. So measure a little more than you'll probably need—and learn to recognize when the dough looks, feels, and acts right at each stage.

To measure flour accurately, stir it a bit in the container, lightly spoon it into a cup designed for measuring dry ingredients, and then level it off with a straight-edged knife. In bread making, there is no need to sift flour. On the other hand, you should never pack it in the cup or shake it down.

Liquids in bread always include at least ¼ cup warm water for dissolving the yeast. Temperature here is crucial: if the water is too cool, the yeast action will be sluggish; if it is too hot, it will destroy the yeast and the dough will fail to rise. For active dry yeast, the water should be about 110°—noticeably warm but not hot. For compressed yeast, it should be about 95°—close to skin temperature. Test with a candy thermometer until you can recognize the right warmth by feel.

Besides water, various other liquids are often mixed into bread, each imparting a distinctive flavor and texture. Milk (also warmed to 95° or 110°) creates a velvety grain; eggs (at room temperature), beaten and used as part of the liquid, lend the loaf a richness, tenderness, and slightly golden tone. Both milk and eggs, of course, also enrich the bread with added nutrients. Occasionally, fruit juice is used in bread to give it a special flavor. Bread made entirely with water (French bread is an example) is distinctively coarse-textured, chewy, and crusty.

Sugar provides food for the yeast so it can grow, while **salt** slows down the action of the yeast, keeping the dough on just the right leavening schedule for good texture and flavor. Besides their purely chemical

role, both salt and sugar are essential for good taste. Also, the sugar in bread helps to brown the crust.

Like liquids, different sweeteners create different flavors. Granulated sugar is commonly used in white bread; brown sugar, honey, and molasses are often used in dark breads to bring out their more robust flavor. As you experiment, substituting honey or molasses for granular sugar, reduce the other liquid in the recipe by an equal amount.

Fats make breads tender, moist, and palatable. Salad oil is convenient to use, because in most recipes the fat is added in liquid form. However, many bakers prefer to use melted butter or margarine because they contribute such rich flavor. For soft, shiny crusts, brush loaves with butter as soon as you take them from the oven.

Special ingredients, such as herbs, spices, cheese, dried fruits, and nuts, offer the bread baker a wide field for experimentation. They aren't essential to the basic creation, but they can be exciting additions for special flavors—and there's usually no need to adjust the proportions of the other ingredients.

Making a Promising Dough

The secret to a shapely, springy loaf of bread is the care and thoroughness given to mixing and kneading the dough. These are the steps that develop the gluten in the flour.

Mixing

In most recipes, the yeast is dissolved first, then other ingredients are mixed in, the flour last of all. A large, heavy pottery bowl is ideal for mixing the dough. It retains warmth and remains steady during beating (especially if you set it on a damp cloth). But don't let the lack of a pottery bowl discourage you from trying bread—any bowl of about 4-quart size will do.

It is also helpful to the yeast if your kitchen is warm, but this, too, is not essential; in a cool kitchen the dough will just take a bit longer to rise. Make sure, though, that the dough is kept away from drafts.

When you add the flour, sprinkle it over the yeast mixture 1 cup at a time, stirring until evenly moistened. When enough flour has been stirred in to form a thick batter (about ⅔ the amount given in a recipe), beat the batter very well with a wooden spoon or with a heavy-duty electric mixer on medium speed. After you have beaten for about 5 minutes, you can see the gluten developing—the batter becomes glossy and elastic, stretching with the motion of the spoon. From this point on, it readily absorbs more flour and tends to stick to itself rather than to you, gradually forming a ball.

By hand, stir in enough of the remaining flour to make a dough stiff enough to pull away from the sides of the bowl.

Kneading

Spread about ½ cup flour on a board, heavily coating the center area. Turn the dough out onto this area and sprinkle it lightly with flour. Now the dough is ready for kneading, which will complete the gluten formation.

As you knead, make sure the dough is never without a light coating of flour. Your objective is to shape it into a ball, keeping the underside smooth and unbroken.

Contrary to popular belief, kneading is not a very good way to work off frustrations—frequency, rhythm, and a *gentle* touch, rather than brute force, do the job best.

To knead, reach under the edge of dough farthest from you. Pull it toward you in a rolling motion (don't pull enough to tear the surface) and fold the dough almost in half. Then, with your finger tips or the heel of your palm, gently roll the ball away from you to lightly seal the fold. When the fold line is returned to the top center of the dough, rotate the dough a quarter turn and continue this folding-rolling motion, making a turn each time. Work quickly, for dough grows sticky if allowed to stand. Spread more flour onto the board gradually as needed for easy handling. If tears occur on the surface, try to fold them in rather than add more flour to cover them; if the dough sticks to the board, lift it up, scrape the board clean, reflour, and continue.

If you work quickly, 5 minutes of kneading may be long enough. But it is virtually impossible to overknead, and the longer you spend at it (perhaps 20 or 30 minutes), the higher and fluffier your finished loaf is likely to be. Again, it's best to judge by feel. When the dough becomes smooth and no longer sticky, its surface faintly pebbled with air bubbles, hold it to your cheek. If it has the firm bounce and velvety touch of a baby's bottom, you have kneaded it long enough.

If you have mixed your dough in a heavy-duty mixer with a dough hook, all this will go much more quickly. Use the criteria of appearance and feel mentioned above to judge when the dough has been kneaded long enough.

Letting it rise

After the dough has been thoroughly kneaded, it almost takes care of itself. Your job is to give it a warm (about 80°), draft-free place for rising—sometimes called "proofing." Most yeast breads rise twice, the first time until doubled in bulk and the second time until almost doubled.

For the first rising, turn the dough over in a greased bowl (the wiped-out mixing bowl will do nicely) to grease it all over. Cover it with a damp cloth or clear plastic wrap (the latter will keep it a bit warmer). In most households, the most convenient warm place to leave the dough is the inside of a switched-off oven. If your oven feels cool, turn it to the lowest setting for

a minute or two, then switch it off before putting the bread inside.

Like so many aspects of bread making, rising times are variable, depending mainly on temperature but also on the heaviness of the dough (whole grain breads take longer than white breads). If the dough looks doubled after the length of time suggested in the recipe, check it by poking two fingers into it. If the indentations remain, the dough has risen enough.

Turn it out onto a lightly floured board and knead briefly to release air bubbles. At this point, you divide and shape the dough as the recipe specifies. To shape a conventional loaf, see Step 8 of the Basic White Bread recipe on page 9. Other loaf and roll shapes are described under *What Shape Shall I Bake?* on page 21 as well as under *Bread Sculpture* on page 61.

After putting the loaves in greased pans, you cover them and let them rise again as you did the dough in the bowl. This step usually takes about half as long as the first rising. Use the same test for readiness as you did after the first rising: make a slight dent in the dough where it is least likely to show. If the indentation remains, the bread is ready for the oven.

Making Bread Fit Your Schedule

A novice baker may feel a bit daunted by all the variables in making yeast bread, as well as by the length of time it takes. Suppose you are interrupted? Or suppose you want to bake yeast bread but don't have quite enough time to get through all the steps in a single day?

Don't worry about short interruptions—up to half an hour. If you have just dissolved the yeast, cover it and leave it at room temperature. It won't hurt it to ferment for awhile. If you are mixing or kneading the dough, cover it to keep it from drying out.

Should it be inconvenient to shape the loaves when the dough has doubled in bulk, just punch it down and let it rise again. You can punch it down two or three times and still bake excellent bread. Watch closely, though—each successive rising will take a little less time.

If you happen to leave the dough too long so that it rises too high (becomes "overproofed"), the solution is to punch it down, knead it a bit to release air, and let it rise again. Overproofed dough looks as though it has ballooned beyond double its original size. Its "skin" is thin and transparent, with bubbles just beneath the surface. If left long enough, it may deflate itself; just punch it down and let it rise again.

You can postpone the last steps—shaping, second rising, and baking—by leaving the dough, covered with clear plastic wrap, in the refrigerator for several hours. The rising action will continue, but at a much slower pace. When you're ready, let the dough finish rising, covered, in a warm place. Several recipes in

Flour and Other Grain Products

Over the ages, bread has been made from a fascinating array of different grains. Wherever climate and soil allowed its cultivation, wheat has been the mainstay—no doubt because of its gluten content, which makes bread dough elastic enough to rise when leavened. But other grains, in proper proportions, blend happily with wheat in bread, contributing special flavors and textures.

All-purpose flour (regular white flour) is a blend of refined wheat flours especially suitable for making bread. It is available either bleached or unbleached—the latter is stronger and creates a better texture. It consists mainly of the starchy interior (called "endosperm") of the wheat kernel, after the bran and germ have been removed and vitamins and minerals added. Because it makes a relatively light dough, it is often combined with heavier whole grain flours to improve texture.

Gluten flour is wheat flour that has been treated to remove nearly all the starch, leaving a very high gluten content. Since gluten is the protein in wheat that makes dough elastic, you can successfully combine a higher ratio of gluten flour with nonglutenous flours (such as soy flour) than you could all-purpose flour. Buy it at health food stores.

Whole wheat flour, ground from the entire wheat kernel, is heavier, richer in nutrients, and more perishable than all-purpose flour. Unless you use it up quickly, store it in the refrigerator to prevent the wheat germ in it from becoming rancid. Many people prefer stone-ground whole wheat to regularly milled whole wheat, because it is slightly coarser and has a heartier flavor.

Graham flour, named for Dr. Sylvester Graham, who developed it in the last century, is practically indistinguishable from regular whole wheat flour. It is stone-ground, and it contains noticeable flecks of coarse bran.

Unprocessed bran and **wheat germ** are portions of the wheat kernel sometimes added in small quantities to breads for nutritional enrichment, heartiness, and special flavors. Both are much coarser than flour. Bran contributes roughage; wheat germ is rich in food value (B and E vitamins, certain proteins, iron, and fat).

Cracked wheat, also much coarser than flour, results when wheat kernels are cut into angular fragments. In small additions, it gives whole grain breads a nutty flavor and crunchy texture.

Rye is available in most markets as dark or light flour and in some health food stores as a meal. Rye has long been a staple in northern Europe and Russia, since it is a less chancy crop than wheat in cold climates. Because it is glutenous (though less so than wheat) the two grains are often combined.

Cornmeal and oatmeal come, respectively, from coarsely ground white or yellow corn and from rolled or steel-cut oats. In some recipes one or the other is combined in small quantities with wheat flour to create distinctive flavors and textures. Corn and oat flours are less widely available; check with health food stores (for corn flour you might also check markets that carry Mexican products).

this chapter are especially formulated for longer refrigeration: Refrigerator Bread, page 11; Onion-Herb Hot Dog Buns, page 28; and Peda Bread I, page 44.

Other recipes to try if you are short of time are any of the batter breads on pages 11 through 13.

Freezing and Reheating

Bread freezes beautifully for as long as 3 months. Usually, freezing is the best way to assure fresh-baked flavor if you have turned out a number of loaves on a bountiful day—or even if you have made only two. Even wrapped airtight, most bread stays fresh for only a few days in the refrigerator or bread box (some loaves grow stale faster, some last a bit longer, depending on ingredients).

As soon as you take the bread from the oven, turn it out of its pan to cool on a wire rack, unless otherwise directed in the recipe. If you plan to serve it soon, let it cool for 10 to 15 minutes before slicing. If you want to freeze it, let it cool completely, wrap each loaf airtight in foil, then package in a plastic bag, label, and place it in the freezer.

To serve frozen bread, unwrap but leave partially covered, and let it thaw completely at room temperature before serving or reheating. You can reheat the thawed bread by placing it on a baking sheet in a 350° oven for about 15 minutes for rolls and small loaves, 30 minutes for large loaves. If it has a soft crust, protect it during reheating with a loose wrapping of foil; if the bread is crusty, reheat it uncovered.

Basic White Bread—Ten Steps to Fresh-baked Goodness

Here's an excellent first recipe to try if you are a novice to yeast bread baking. On these two pages you'll find photographs of what to expect at each stage, as well as detailed directions about what to do.

For this basic recipe, you'll need two 9 by 5-inch bread pans, either metal or glass. You'll also need about 6 cups of flour, but measure an amount well in excess of this into a large bowl for convenience in dipping it out as you need it.

To measure, first stir the flour a few times, then spoon it lightly into a measuring cup and level it off with a spatula or straight-edged knife. Heat the milk to about 110° (check with a candy thermometer until you learn to recognize the temperature by feel).

To make one loaf of bread from the basic recipe, halve all the ingredients *except* the yeast and warm water.

¼ cup warm water (about 110°)
1 package active dry yeast
2 cups warm milk (about 110°)
2 tablespoons butter or margarine, melted and
    cooled (or use salad oil)
2 teaspoons salt
2 tablespoons granulated sugar
6 to 6½ cups all-purpose flour, unsifted

Step 1. Pour water into bowl; add yeast and stir until dissolved. Add milk, butter, salt, and sugar; stir until well blended.

Step 5. Put dough in greased bowl; turn over to grease top. Cover bowl with clear plastic wrap or damp cloth. Let rise in warm place (80°) until doubled (about 1½ hours). Test by inserting 2 fingers into dough—if indentations remain, dough is ready to shape.

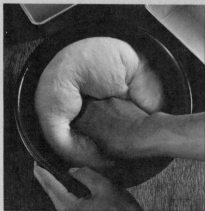

Step 6. After dough has risen, punch it down to release air bubbles, then turn dough out onto a lightly floured board. Knead dough briefly and shape into a smooth oval.

Step 7. To divide dough in half for 2 loaves, grasp dough in center and squeeze. Then form each half into a loaf by gently pulling top surface toward underside to make top smooth.

Step 2. Sprinkle in 3 cups of the flour, 1 cup at a time, stirring until flour is evenly moistened. Add 4th cup of flour and beat until dough is smooth and elastic (about 5 minutes—rest when you get tired). Mix in 5th cup of flour to make a stiff dough.

Step 3. Measure 6th cup of flour; sprinkle about half of it on board. Turn dough out onto heavily floured area of board. Keep a light coating of flour on dough as you begin to knead.

Step 4. Fold dough toward you with your fingers; push away with heel of your hand. Rotate dough a quarter turn and repeat folding-pushing motion, adding flour to board as you knead. Kneading is finished when dough is nonsticky, smooth, and satiny.

Step 8. Turn each loaf over in one hand and with your other hand, pinch a seam down center, then turn ends, and pinch to seal as shown.

Step 9. Put shaped loaves, seam side down, in greased 9 by 5-inch loaf pans. Cover; let rise in warm place until almost doubled (about 45 minutes).

Step 10. Bake in a 375° oven (350° for glass pans) for about 45 minutes or until loaves are nicely browned and sound hollow when tapped. Remove from oven; turn loaves out of pans onto racks to cool before slicing or wrapping.

Herb Breads

Follow Basic White Bread recipe (page 8). If you want to make 2 kinds, in Step 4 divide dough into 2 parts; knead each part separately, kneading a different herb into each. Select from these herbs, using the following amounts for *each half* of the dough: 1 tablespoon **dill weed**, 1 tablespoon **savory**, 1½ teaspoons dry **basil**, 1½ teaspoons **oregano leaves**, 1½ teaspoons **thyme**, or 2¼ teaspoons **marjoram**.

Poppy Seed Bubble Loaf

Follow Basic White Bread recipe (page 8) with these changes: In Steps 7 through 10, after dough is punched down, pinch off pieces of dough to make tiny balls (about 1 inch in diameter). Melt 4 tablespoons **butter** or margarine. Measure ¼ cup **poppy seed**. Dip top of each ball first into butter, then into poppy seed, and pile all the balls, seed side up, in one lightly greased 10-inch tube pan; cover and let rise. Bake in a 375° oven for about 55 minutes or until nicely browned.

Cinnamon Swirl Loaf

Follow Basic White Bread recipe (page 8) except in Steps 8 and 9, roll out dough for each loaf into a rectangle about 6 by 16 inches. Mix 4 tablespoons **sugar** with 4 tablespoons ground **cinnamon**; sprinkle half evenly over top of each rectangle. Beginning with a narrow side, roll each tightly into a loaf; seal ends and bottom by pinching together to make seam. Let rise in 2 greased 9 by 5-inch pans. Bake in a 375° oven for 30 to 35 minutes or until nicely browned.

Egg Braid

Follow Basic White Bread recipe (page 8) except in Step 1, break 2 **eggs** into a 2-cup measure; beat in enough warm **milk** to make 2 cups, and use this mixture in place of all milk. In Step 8, divide dough for *each loaf* into 3 parts; roll each into a strand. Braid each trio of strands together, pinching ends to seal. In Step 9, let rise on lightly greased baking sheet. Brush with slightly beaten **egg** before baking. Bake in a 375° oven for 30 to 35 minutes or until nicely browned.

Crust Treatments

How do you like your crust—tender to the bite or thick, chewy, and challenging? You can achieve a wide spectrum of textures, tastes, and tones, using different glazes and a few baker's tricks.

For a chewy-crisp crust like that of French bread, place a pan of water on the rack below the bread as it bakes. The steam encircling the bread in the hot oven does the trick.

Brushing with a simple **cornstarch and water mixture** also helps to create a chewy crust and gives the loaf a glossy tone. Dissolve 1 teaspoon **cornstarch** in ⅔ cup **water**; heat the mixture in a pan until boiling. Cool slightly and, with a soft brush, paint the loaf just before baking. After baking it for 10 minutes, remove the bread and paint it again.

Egg glazes make bread lustrous and golden, and because they are sticky, they come in handy for keeping poppy or sesame seeds in place. Just before baking, paint the bread with one lightly beaten whole **egg**—or use either one **yolk** or one **white** beaten with a tablespoon of cold **water**.

If tenderness is your preference, brush loaves with melted **butter or margarine** just before baking or as soon as you take them from the oven. For a slightly different soft crust, brush with **milk or cream** before baking.

Dutch crunch is a yeast and rice flour topping that makes bread delightfully crunchy and crackled. You can find the rice flour in some markets and most health food stores (don't confuse it with Oriental rice flour, which is also called "sweet rice flour").

Here's how to make Dutch crunch topping for two loaves or one and a half dozen rolls: Stir together 1½ tablespoons **sugar**, 4 packages **active dry yeast**, ½ teaspoon **salt**, and ¾ cup **rice flour**. Add 2 teaspoons **salad oil** and ½ to ⅔ cup warm **water** (about 110°); stir to blend well and form a thick paste. Cover and let rise in a warm place until doubled and very bubbly (about 30 minutes). Stir down. If necessary, topping can stand, covered, at room temperature another 15 minutes; then stir again.

Meanwhile, shape dough into loaves or rolls. Spread topping evenly over tops and down sides of rolls or loaves. Cover very lightly with clear plastic wrap. Let rise, remove plastic, and bake as recipe directs.

Oatmeal Bread

Follow Basic White Bread recipe (page 8), using 4 cups **all-purpose flour** and 2 cups **oat flour** (both unsifted). Oat flour is found in health food stores—or make it by whirling rolled oats in electric blender until fine.

Dark Mixed Grain Bread

Follow Basic White Bread recipe (page 8), but omit sugar; instead of all milk, use ½ cup dark **molasses** with 1½ cups **milk**. Omit all-purpose flour and use ½ cup **wheat germ**, ½ cup **buckwheat flour**, 1 cup **rye flour**, and 4 cups **whole wheat flour** (all unsifted).

Rye Bread

Follow Basic White Bread recipe (page 8), but in Step 1, omit sugar; instead of all milk, use ½ cup light or dark **molasses** with 1½ cups **milk**. Use 3 cups **rye flour** and 3 cups **all-purpose flour** (both unsifted).

Super Simple Refrigerator Bread

Here is a light and tender white loaf to try when you're pressed for time. It couldn't be easier—there's no kneading, and it waits in the refrigerator for as long as 24 hours.

- ⅓ cup *each* sugar and shortening
- 1 tablespoon salt
- 2 cups boiling water
- 2 packages active dry yeast
- 1 teaspoon sugar
- ¼ cup warm water (about 110°)
- 2 eggs, well beaten
- 7½ to 8 cups all-purpose flour, unsifted

In a large bowl, combine the ⅓ cup sugar, shortening, salt, and boiling water; cool to lukewarm. Dissolve yeast and the 1 teaspoon sugar in the ¼ cup water; set in warm place until bubbly (about 15 minutes).

Combine yeast mixture with lukewarm mixture; stir in eggs. Beat in 4 cups of the flour; then gradually stir in as much of the remaining flour as dough will absorb, mixing well. Place in a greased bowl; cover and chill for at least 3 hours or up to 24 hours.

To bake, divide dough in half. With greased hands, shape each half into a smooth loaf. Place each in a

greased 9 by 5-inch loaf pan; cover and let rise in a warm place until almost doubled (about 2 hours).

Bake in a 350° oven for 30 to 35 minutes or until bread sounds hollow when tapped. Let cool on racks. Makes 2 loaves.

Rich White Batter Bread

Coffee cans give this moist, fine-textured bread its distinctive shape—tall, round, and domed. The plastic lids that come with the cans prove useful, too, at several different stages. First, they seal the batter in the can for freezing if you want to bake the bread another time. Next, the lids tell you when the dough (which rises only once) is ready to bake—they pop off. And once the baked loaf is sliced below the top of the can, the lid will seal it in to keep it fresh.

- 1 package active dry yeast
- ½ cup warm water (about 110°)
- ⅛ teaspoon ground ginger
- 3 tablespoons sugar
- 1 large can (13 oz.) evaporated milk
- 1 teaspoon salt
- 2 tablespoons salad oil
- 4 to 4½ cups all-purpose flour, unsifted
  Butter or margarine

In a large bowl, dissolve yeast in water; blend in ginger and 1 tablespoon of the sugar. Let stand in a warm place until bubbly (about 15 minutes). Stir in remaining 2 tablespoons sugar, the milk, salt, and oil. Gradually beat in enough of the flour, 1 cup at a time, to make batter very heavy and stiff, but too sticky to knead.

Spoon batter into a well-greased 2-pound coffee can, or divide in half and place in 2 well-greased 1-pound coffee cans. Cover with greased plastic can lids. Freeze if you wish.

To bake, let covered cans stand in a warm place until batter rises and pops off plastic lids (45 to 55 minutes for 1-pound cans, 55 to 60 minutes for 2-pound cans).

(Continued on next page)

If frozen, let batter stand in cans at room temperature until lids pop (4 to 5 hours for 1-pound cans, 6 to 8 hours for 2-pound cans).

Bake in a 350° oven for about 45 minutes for 1-pound cans, about 60 minutes for a 2-pound can; crust will be very brown. Brush tops lightly with butter. Let cool in cans on a rack for 10 minutes; then loosen crust around edge of can with a thin knife, slide bread from can, and let cool in an upright position on rack. Makes 1 large or 2 small loaves.

Light Wheat Bread

Follow Rich White Batter Bread recipe (page 11), but replace sugar with 3 tablespoons **honey**. Use 1½ cups **whole wheat flour** and 3 cups **all-purpose flour** (both unsifted).

Corn-Herb Batter Bread

Follow Rich White Batter Bread recipe (page 11), adding to yeast mixture 2 teaspoons **celery seed**, 1½ teaspoons ground **sage**, and ⅛ teaspoon **marjoram**. Substitute ½ cup yellow **cornmeal** for ½ cup of the flour.

Raisin-Nut Batter Bread

Follow Rich White Batter Bread recipe (page 11), adding to yeast mixture 1 teaspoon ground **cinnamon** and ½ teaspoon ground **nutmeg**. Stir ½ cup *each* **raisins** and chopped **walnuts** into batter with final addition of flour.

Three Wheat Batter Bread

Hearty, nutritious ingredients go into this batter bread. Wheat germ and cracked wheat add a nutty flavor and give the bread a pleasing, crunchy texture. (*Photograph on page 22.*)

- 1 package active dry yeast
- ½ cup warm water (about 110°)
- ⅛ teaspoon ground ginger
- 3 tablespoons honey
- 1 large can (13 oz.) evaporated milk
- 1 teaspoon salt
- 2 tablespoons salad oil
- 2½ cups all-purpose flour, unsifted
- 1¼ cups whole wheat flour, unsifted
- ½ cup wheat germ
- ¼ cup cracked wheat

In a large bowl, combine yeast, water, ginger, and 1 tablespoon of the honey; let stand in a warm place until bubbly (about 20 minutes). Stir in remaining honey, milk, salt, and oil. Stir together all-purpose flour, whole wheat flour, wheat germ, and cracked wheat; add to liquid ingredients, 1 cup at a time, beating after each addition until well blended.

Spoon batter evenly into a well-greased 2-pound coffee can or into 2 well-greased 1-pound coffee cans; cover with greased plastic lids. Freeze if you wish.

Let rise in a warm place until lids pop off (about 55 to 60 minutes for 1-pound cans, 1 to 1½ hours for 2-pound cans). *If frozen*, follow rising directions given for Rich White Batter Bread (page 11).

Bake, uncovered, in a 350° oven for about 45 minutes for 1-pound cans, about 60 minutes for a 2-pound can, or until bread sounds hollow when tapped. Let cool in cans on racks for 10 minutes; then loosen crust around edge of can with a thin knife, slide bread from can, and let cool in an upright position on rack. Makes 1 large or 2 small loaves.

Cheddar Cheese and Caraway Bread

Time-conscious bread bakers will appreciate the quick, no-knead method used to make this Cheddar-flavored batter bread. A Parmesan-dill seed variation follows this recipe.

Slice these breads thinly to serve with cold ham or roast beef in sandwiches, or with any luncheon or dinner menu.

- 1 large can (13 oz.) evaporated milk
- 3 tablespoons sugar
- 3 tablespoons butter or margarine, cut in pieces
- 2 teaspoons *each* salt and caraway seed
- ½ teaspoon garlic powder
- 1½ cups (about 6 oz.) shredded sharp Cheddar cheese
- 1 package active dry yeast
- ¼ cup warm water (about 110°)
- 3¾ cups all-purpose flour, unsifted
- 2 eggs

In a pan, combine milk, sugar, butter, salt, caraway seed, garlic powder, and cheese. Heat, stirring, to about 110° (butter and cheese need not melt completely).

In a large bowl, dissolve yeast in the ¼ cup water. Add milk mixture; beat in 1½ cups of the flour. Add eggs, 1 at a time, beating well after each addition; gradually beat in 1½ cups more flour until batter is smooth. With a spoon, beat in remaining ¾ cup flour. Cover and let rise in a warm place until doubled (about 45 minutes).

Stir batter down and spoon into a generously greased 10-inch tube pan or two 4½ by 8½-inch loaf pans. Cover and let rise in a warm place until almost doubled (about 45 minutes).

Bake in a 350° oven for about 55 minutes (45 minutes for loaf pans) or until bread sounds hollow when tapped. Let cool in pan on rack for 10 minutes; then turn out onto rack to cool completely. Makes 1 large or 2 small loaves.

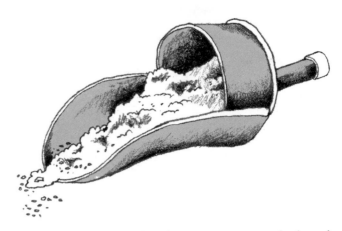

Parmesan Cheese and Dill Bread

Follow recipe for Cheddar Cheese and Caraway Bread (above), omitting Cheddar cheese, caraway seed, and garlic powder. Instead, use 1 cup grated **Parmesan cheese,** 3 tablespoons instant minced **onion,** and 3 teaspoons **dill seed.**

Orange-Rye Batter Bread

Orange peel gives this rye batter bread a Scandinavian touch. As with many of the batter breads, you let the dough rise in coffee cans, but just until it pushes up against the lids—not until they pop off.

    1 package active dry yeast
    ½ cup warm water (about 110°)
    ⅛ teaspoon ground ginger
    1 tablespoon sugar
    3 tablespoons light molasses
    1 teaspoon *each* caraway seed (optional) and
        salt
    1 tablespoon grated orange peel
    2 tablespoons salad oil
    1 large can (13 oz.) evaporated milk
    1½ cups rye flour, unsifted
    3 cups all-purpose flour, unsifted
        Butter or margarine

In a large bowl, dissolve yeast in water; blend in ginger and sugar. Let stand in a warm place until bubbly (about 15 minutes). Stir in molasses, caraway seed, salt, orange peel, oil, and milk. Add flours, 1 cup at a time, beating well after each addition until batter is smooth. Batter will be very stiff, but too sticky to knead.

Spoon batter into a well-greased 2-pound coffee can, or divide in half and place in 2 well-greased 1-pound coffee cans. Cover with greased plastic lids. Freeze if you wish.

Let rise in a warm place just until batter pushes up against can lids (40 to 45 minutes for 1-pound cans, 55 to 60 minutes for a 2-pound can). *If frozen,* follow rising directions given in Rich White Batter Bread recipe (page 11). Remove lids.

Bake in a 350° oven for about 45 minutes for 1-pound cans, about 60 minutes for 2-pound can. Brush tops lightly with butter. Let cool in cans on a

rack for 10 minutes; then loosen crust around edge of can with a thin knife, slide bread from can, and let cool in an upright position on rack. Makes 1 large or 2 small loaves.

Whole Grain Cereal Bread

This baked-in-a-coffee-can batter bread gets its distinctive flavor and texture from whole grain cereal. For variety, you have a choice of several kinds of cereal—quick-cooking wheat cereal, rolled oats, or a mixed grain cereal. Each gives a slightly different character to the loaf.

    1 package active dry yeast
    ½ cup warm water (about 110°)
    2 tablespoons molasses
    1 teaspoon salt
    1 egg, slightly beaten
    1 cup milk
    2 tablespoons butter or margarine
    1 cup whole grain cereal (see above),
        uncooked
    3½ cups all-purpose flour, unsifted

In a large bowl, dissolve yeast in water. Stir in molasses, salt, and egg. In a pan, heat milk and butter to about 110° (butter need not melt completely). Add milk mixture to yeast, then blend in cereal. Gradually beat in flour to make a smooth, elastic batter; it will be very stiff, but too sticky to knead.

Spoon batter into a well-greased 2-pound coffee can or into 2 well-greased 1-pound coffee cans; cover with greased plastic lids. Freeze if you wish.

Let rise in a warm place until lid pops off (about 40 to 45 minutes for 1-pound cans, 55 to 60 minutes for 2-pound can). *If frozen,* follow rising directions given in Rich White Batter Bread recipe (page 11).

Bake in a 350° oven for about 45 minutes for 1-pound cans, about 60 minutes for a 2-pound can; crust will be well browned. Let cool in can on a rack for 10 minutes; then loosen crust around edge of can with a thin knife, slide bread from can, and let cool in an upright position on rack. Makes 1 large or 2 small loaves.

Short-cut Yeast Dough Mix and Six Ways to Use It

This short-cut bread mix will be a real timesaver if you bake yeast breads on a fairly regular basis. You start by mixing a 5-pound bag of flour—either white or whole wheat—with salt, sugar, and nonfat dry milk; then you store the mixture until you decide it's time to bake.

If you keep it tightly sealed, your bread mix will keep almost indefinitely; since you add the yeast later, there's no worry about its becoming outdated.

When you're ready to bake, measure out some of this mix and add it to the yeast, egg, and oil to make any of the delicious breads offered in the recipes that follow; one batch of mix is enough for all six.

    1 bag (5 lb.) all-purpose or whole wheat
         flour (both unsifted)
  2½ tablespoons salt
    1 cup sugar
    2 cups nonfat dry milk

In a large bowl, stir together until thoroughly blended the flour, salt, sugar, and milk. Seal in tightly covered containers or in heavy plastic bags and store in a cool place or refrigerate; mixture will keep almost indefinitely. Stir well before each use.

To use stone-ground whole wheat flour: Prepare as directed above, except use a 5-pound bag of stone-ground whole wheat flour (unsifted) *plus* about 4 extra cups. Measure total number of cups in the bag by spooning flour into cup, then leveling off. Add enough additional flour (about 4 cups) to make a total of 20 cups.

Basic Loaf

    1 package active dry yeast
    1 cup warm water (about 110°)
    2 tablespoons butter or margarine, melted
         and cooled (or use salad oil)
    1 egg
  3½ cups Short-cut Yeast Dough Mix
         About ½ cup all-purpose flour, unsifted

Dissolve yeast in water; stir in butter and egg. Add yeast dough mix to yeast mixture and stir until well blended. Turn dough out onto a floured board and knead until smooth and satiny (5 to 20 minutes), adding flour as needed to prevent sticking. Turn dough over in a greased bowl; cover and let rise in a warm place until doubled (about 1½ hours).

Punch dough down and knead briefly on a lightly floured board to release air. Shape into a smooth loaf and place in a greased 9 by 5-inch loaf pan. Cover and let rise in a warm place until almost doubled (30 to 45 minutes).

Bake in a 350° oven for about 30 minutes or until loaf is nicely browned and sounds hollow when tapped. Turn out onto rack to cool. Makes 1 loaf.

Cardamom Raisin Loaf. Prepare Basic Loaf as directed, adding 1½ teaspoons ground **cardamom** and ½ cup **raisins** with the egg. When time to shape, form dough into a smooth ball and place in a greased 9-inch pie pan. Cover, let rise, and bake as directed for Basic Loaf. While still warm, drizzle with this icing: stir together ½ cup unsifted **powered sugar**, 1 tablespoon **milk**, and ½ teaspoon **orange extract or vanilla**. Decorate with sliced **almonds**.

Onion Pan Rolls. Prepare Basic Loaf as directed, adding 2 single-serving-size packages **onion soup mix** with the egg. (If using yeast dough mix made with stone-ground whole wheat flour, increase water by 2 tablespoons.) When time to shape, divide dough into 18 equal pieces. Shape each into a ball and arrange in 2 greased 8-inch round cake pans. Cover and let rise until almost doubled (about 50 minutes). Bake in a 350° oven for 25 minutes or until browned. *(Photograph on page 19.)*

Arrange balls of dough in greased 8-inch round cake pan.

Pizza Crust. Prepare Basic Loaf as directed, but increase water to 1¼ cups and omit egg. When time to shape, divide dough in half and roll each to fit a greased 14-inch pizza pan, building up edge slightly. (Or wrap and freeze half the dough; to use, let warm to room temperature.) Do not let dough rise a second time. Adjust oven racks so they are evenly spaced from top to bottom. *(Photograph on page 19.)*

Bake crusts in a 450° oven for about 10 minutes or until lightly browned (switch pans halfway through baking). Remove from oven and spread with your favorite sauce and toppings. Return to oven and bake for about 10 minutes longer or until topping is bubbly (switch pans halfway through baking).

Herb Cheese Ring. Prepare Basic Loaf as directed, adding 2 teaspoons instant toasted **onion** and either 2 teaspoons **dill weed**, 1½ teaspoons **oregano leaves**, or 1½ teaspoons dry **basil** with the egg. When time to shape, roll out dough into a 10 by 18-inch rectangle. Sprinkle evenly with 1 cup shredded **Cheddar cheese** (pack into cup) and ¼ cup grated **Parmesan cheese**.

Starting at a wide end, roll up jelly-roll fashion; pinch seam to seal. Place roll, seam side down, on a greased baking sheet and shape into a ring. Pinch ends together to seal. With a razor blade or a sharp

floured knife, make slashes about ½ inch deep and about 2 inches apart on top of ring. Cover and let rise until almost doubled (about 50 minutes). Brush ring evenly with 1 **egg yolk** mixed with 2 teaspoons **water**; sprinkle with 1 tablespoon grated **Parmesan cheese**. Bake as for Basic Loaf. *(Photograph on page 19.)*

Cinnamon Swirl Loaf. Prepare Basic Loaf as directed. Combine ¼ cup *each* **sugar** and chopped **walnuts** and 1½ teaspoons ground **cinnamon.** When time to shape, roll dough out into an 8 by 18-inch rectangle. Brush with 1 tablespoon melted **butter** or margarine and sprinkle with cinnamon-nut mixture.

Starting at a narrow end, roll dough up tightly and pinch seams to seal. Place seam side down in a greased 9 by 5-inch loaf pan; cover and let rise until almost doubled (about 1 hour and 15 minutes). Bake as directed for Basic Loaf. While still warm, drizzle with this icing: stir together ½ cup unsifted **powdered sugar**, 1 tablespoon **milk**, and ½ teaspoon **orange extract or vanilla**. *(Photograph on page 19.)*

How to shape Herb Cheese Ring

1. Sprinkle cheese evenly over rolled-out dough.

2. Starting from wide side, roll up jelly-roll fashion; pinch seam together to seal.

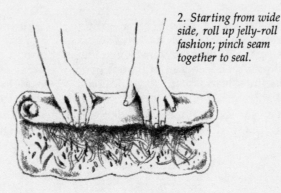

3. Shape roll into a ring, pinching ends to seal; place, seam side down, on ungreased baking sheet.

4. Slash top of ring, making cuts ½ inch deep and 2 inches apart, using razor blade or sharp floured knife.

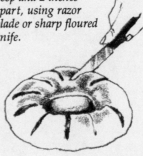

Pebble-top Oatmeal Bread

An attractive pebble topping of rolled oats adorns this even-textured bread. It makes wholesome breakfast toast, delicious with butter and honey or your favorite jam. *(Photograph on page 22.)*

- 1 package active dry yeast
- ¼ cup warm water (about 110°)
- ¼ cup molasses
- ¼ cup butter or margarine
- 2 teaspoons salt
- ¼ cup firmly packed brown sugar
- 2½ cups regular or quick-cooking rolled oats
- 1 cup *each* boiling water and cold water
- 4½ to 5 cups all-purpose flour, unsifted
- 3 tablespoons milk

In a small bowl, combine yeast, warm water, and 1 tablespoon of the molasses; let stand until bubbly (about 15 minutes). In a large bowl, combine butter, remaining molasses, salt, sugar, 2 cups of the oats, and boiling water; stir until butter melts; add cold water and yeast mixture. Beat in 4 cups of the flour, 1 cup at a time.

Turn dough out onto a floured board; knead until smooth and elastic (10 to 20 minutes), adding flour as needed to prevent sticking. Turn dough over in a greased bowl; cover and let rise in a warm place until doubled (about 1 hour).

Punch dough down; knead briefly on a lightly floured board to release air. Divide in half and shape each half into a loaf; place in greased 9 by 5-inch loaf pans. Soften remaining rolled oats in milk; dot over tops. Cover; let rise in a warm place until doubled (about 45 minutes).

Bake in a 350° oven for about 1 hour or until bread sounds hollow when tapped. Turn out on a rack to cool. Makes 2 loaves.

Oat Sesame Bread

Toasted sesame seed not only accents the flavor of this bread made with rolled oats—it also gives a delightfully crunchy texture.

- 1 cup regular rolled oats
- 2 cups boiling water
- ½ cup sesame seed
- 1 package active dry yeast
- ½ cup warm water (about 110°)
- ¼ cup *each* dark molasses and dark corn syrup
- 1½ teaspoons salt
- 3 tablespoons butter or margarine, melted
- 4½ to 5 cups all-purpose flour, unsifted

Stir together rolled oats and boiling water in top of a double boiler; cover and cook over simmering water until water in top pan is absorbed (about 1 hour). Transfer oats to a large bowl; let cool. In a dry frying pan over medium heat, stir sesame seed until browned.

Dissolve yeast in the ½ cup water, then add to cooled oats. Stir in molasses, corn syrup, salt, 2 tablespoons of the butter, and sesame seed. Beat in about 4 cups of the flour to make a stiff dough. Turn dough out onto a floured board; knead until smooth and elastic (10 to 20 minutes), adding flour as needed to prevent sticking.

Turn dough over in greased bowl; cover and let rise in a warm place until doubled (about 2 hours). Punch dough down, knead briefly on a lightly floured board to release air, and shape into 2 loaves. Place each loaf in a 4½ by 8½-inch loaf pan, greased on the bottom only. Cover and let rise until almost doubled (about 45 minutes).

Brush tops of loaves with remaining 1 tablespoon butter. Bake in a 400° oven for about 40 minutes or until loaves sound hollow when tapped. Turn out on a rack to cool. Makes 2 loaves.

Sunflower Whole Wheat Bread

Honey gives this bread a rich, sweet flavor and a crisp crust. Stone-ground whole wheat flour and sunflower seeds give it an open-grained texture.

- 1 package active dry yeast
- ⅓ cup warm water (about 110°)
- 2 cups milk, at room temperature
- 3 tablespoons butter or margarine, melted
- 1 tablespoon salt
- ½ cup honey
- 5½ to 6 cups stone-ground whole wheat flour, unsifted
- 1 cup hulled sunflower seeds

In a large bowl, dissolve yeast in water. Add milk, 2 tablespoons of the butter, salt, and honey. Beat in 5 cups of the flour to make a soft dough; stir in sunflower seeds. Turn dough out onto well-floured board; knead until smooth and elastic (10 to 20 minutes), adding flour as needed to prevent sticking. Turn dough over in greased bowl; cover and let rise in a warm place until doubled (about 2 hours).

Punch dough down, knead briefly on a lightly floured board to release air, and shape into 2 loaves. Place each loaf in a 4½ by 8½-inch loaf pan, greased on the bottom only. Cover and let rise until almost doubled (about 45 minutes).

Brush tops of loaves with remaining 1 tablespoon butter. Bake in a 375° oven for about 45 minutes or until loaves are golden brown and sound hollow when tapped. Turn out on a rack to cool. Makes 2 loaves.

Spicy Zucchini Wheat Bread

Hidden shreds of zucchini squash enhance the flavor of this breakfast loaf and give it a moist, even texture. A sprinkling of cardamom and currants makes it delicious, especially when you top it with butter and marmalade.

- ⅔ cup milk
- 3 tablespoons butter or margarine
- 3 tablespoons firmly packed brown sugar or honey
- 1 package active dry yeast
- ¼ cup warm water (about 110°)
- 1½ cups whole wheat flour, unsifted
- 1½ to 2 cups all-purpose flour, unsifted
- ¼ cup wheat germ
- 1 teaspoon *each* salt and grated orange peel
- 2 teaspoons ground cardamom
- 1½ cups coarsely shredded zucchini
- ¾ cup currants or raisins

In a pan, combine milk, butter, and sugar. Heat, stirring, to about 110° (butter need not melt completely).

In a large bowl, dissolve yeast in water; add milk mixture. Stir together whole wheat flour, 1½ cups of the all-purpose flour, wheat germ, salt, orange peel, and cardamom until well blended. Stir about half of this into yeast mixture. Add zucchini and currants; stir to blend. Gradually stir in enough of the remaining flour mixture to make a stiff dough.

Turn dough out onto a well-floured board; knead until smooth and elastic (10 to 20 minutes), adding remaining flour mixture as needed to prevent sticking. Turn dough over in a greased bowl; cover and let rise in a warm place until doubled (about 1½ hours).

Punch dough down; knead briefly on a lightly floured board to release air. Divide in half; shape each half into a smooth ball and place in a greased 1-pound

coffee can (or shape into 2 small loaves and place each in a greased 4½ by 8½-inch loaf pan). Cover and let rise in a warm place until dough rises 1 inch above top of can or doubles in loaf pans (about 45 minutes).

Bake in a 350° oven for 40 to 45 minutes or until tops are dark brown and bread sounds hollow when tapped. Turn out on rack to cool. Makes 2 loaves.

Graham Cracked Wheat Bread

The nutty flavor and texture of this bread comes from cracked wheat. Graham flour can be found in some supermarkets and in most health food stores—or you could substitute whole wheat flour.

- 1 package active dry yeast
- ¼ cup warm water (about 110°)
- 1¾ cups milk, at room temperature
- ¼ cup molasses
- 3 tablespoons butter or margarine, melted
- 2 teaspoons salt
- ¼ cup cracked wheat
- 1½ cups graham flour, unsifted
- 4½ to 5 cups all-purpose flour, unsifted

In a large bowl, dissolve yeast in water. Add milk, molasses, 2 tablespoons of the butter, salt, cracked wheat, and graham flour. Beat in about 4 cups of the all-purpose flour to make a stiff dough. Turn dough out onto a floured board; knead until smooth and elastic, adding flour as needed to prevent sticking. Turn dough over in a greased bowl; cover and let rise in a warm place until doubled (about 2 hours).

Punch dough down, knead briefly on a lightly floured board to release air, and shape into 2 loaves. Place each loaf in a 4½ by 8½-inch loaf pan, greased on the bottom only. Cover and let rise until almost doubled (about 45 minutes).

Brush tops of loaves with remaining 1 tablespoon butter. Bake in a 375° oven for about 45 minutes or until loaves sound hollow when tapped. Turn out on a rack to cool. Makes 2 loaves.

Freezer Whole Wheat Bread

Baking day bounty includes (clockwise from left) Cinnamon Swirl Loaf, Herb Cheese Ring, Onion Pan Rolls, and Pizza, all produced from Short-cut Yeast Dough Mix (page 14).

How better to welcome guests than with the aroma of bread baking? But making bread the day company is coming is more than most of us care to undertake. Here's an alternative. This whole wheat dough is specially formulated (with extra yeast, fat, and sugar) to freeze now and bake later. On the day of your party, you let the shaped dough thaw and rise (about 4 hours)—then it's ready to bake. For variety, you might want to try the rye version of freezer dough, following this recipe.

If you want to make this bread without freezing, use only 1 package of yeast; other ingredients remain the same. Instead of freezing, let the shaped loaves rise until almost doubled, then bake as directed.

1½ **cups milk**
⅓ **cup light molasses**
2 **teaspoons salt**
¼ **cup butter or margarine**
2 **packages active dry yeast**
½ **cup warm water (about 110°)**
5½ **to 6 cups whole wheat flour, unsifted**
 Melted butter or margarine

In a pan, combine milk, molasses, salt, and butter (cut in pieces). Heat to about 110° (butter need not melt completely).

In a large bowl, dissolve yeast in water. Stir in warm milk mixture. Beat in about 5 cups of the flour, 1 cup at a time, to make a stiff dough. Turn dough out onto a floured board; knead until smooth and satiny (5 to 20 minutes), adding flour as needed to prevent sticking. Divide dough in half.

Shape into either standard or round loaves. Place standard loaves in 2 well-greased 4½ by 8½-inch loaf pans; wrap and freeze immediately. Place round loaves on a greased baking sheet; cover, freeze until solid, then wrap each loaf separately and return to freezer.

To bake, remove loaves from freezer (place round loaves on greased baking sheets). Cover loaves with a cloth and let thaw at room temperature (about 2 hours). Let rise, covered, in a warm place until almost doubled (about 2 more hours).

Brush loaves with melted butter and bake in a 375° oven for about 30 minutes or until loaves sound hollow when tapped. Remove from pans and let cool on racks. Makes 2 loaves.

Freezer Rye Bread

Follow recipe for Freezer Whole Wheat Bread (above), substituting ½ cup firmly packed **light brown sugar** for the molasses. Instead of whole wheat flour, use 3 cups **rye flour** and about 3 cups **all-purpose flour** (both unsifted); add 1 tablespoon crushed **fennel seed**. Stir in rye flour, fennel seed, and about 2 cups all-purpose flour. Knead in remaining all-purpose flour, then shape and freeze. Bake as directed for Freezer Whole Wheat Bread, except just before baking, brush loaves with 1 **egg white** beaten with 1 tablespoon **water** and sprinkle each with 1 teaspoon **caraway seed**.

Cracked Wheat Twin-top Bread

Whole grain breads that start from a bubbly sponge of yeast, warm water, sugar, and a bit of flour are distinguished by a pronounced robust flavor and an exceptionally light, even texture.

1 **package active dry yeast**
2½ **cups warm water (about 110°)**
1 **teaspoon granulated sugar**
2 **cups graham flour, unsifted**
½ **cup cracked wheat**
1 **cup warm water (about 110°)**
2 **tablespoons salad oil**
1 **tablespoon salt**
¼ **cup firmly packed brown sugar**
1 **cup** *each* **wheat germ and regular or quick-cooking rolled oats**
2 **tablespoons sesame seed**
5 **to 5½ cups all-purpose flour, unsifted**

In a large bowl, dissolve yeast in the 2½ cups water. Add granulated sugar, graham flour, and cracked wheat. Beat until well combined (about 3 minutes). Let stand in a warm place until bubbly (about 20 minutes).

Stir in the 1 cup warm water, oil, salt, brown sugar, wheat germ, rolled oats, and sesame seed. Beat in about 4 cups of the all-purpose flour to make a stiff dough. Turn dough out onto a floured board; knead until smooth and satiny (5 to 20 minutes), adding flour as needed to prevent sticking.

Turn dough over in a greased bowl; cover and let rise in a warm place until doubled (about 1½ hours). Punch dough down; knead briefly on a lightly floured board to release air. Divide dough into 4 equal portions, shape each into a ball, and place 2 balls side by side in each of 2 greased 9 by 5-inch loaf pans. Cover and let rise until almost doubled (about 45 minutes).

Bake in a 375° oven for 45 minutes or until loaves sound hollow when tapped. Cool in pans for 10 minutes, then turn out on a rack to cool completely. Makes 2 loaves.

Dark Delicatessen Rye Bread

Here's the secret to duplicating those dark delicatessen-style rye breads—unlikely as it may seem, professional bakers deliberately scorch some sugar and then use it to color the bread dough. It's a trick you can easily perform in your own kitchen. You begin by melting sugar as you would for caramel, cook it to a foamy ebony syrup, and then dissolve the charred mass with boiling water.

A word of caution before you start—sugar smokes as it turns black, and when the boiling water is added there will be spattering. Be sure your kitchen is well ventilated (turn on an exhaust fan if available) and protect your hands with oven mitts. When you finish, let the empty pan cool to room temperature, then add hot tap water, soak briefly, and wash as usual. The blackened sugar won't mar the pan. (*Photograph on page 22.*)

    ½ cup sugar
    ¾ cup boiling water
    2 tablespoons solid shortening or butter
    3 packages active dry yeast
    2 cups warm water (about 110°)
    ¼ cup cocoa
    2 teaspoons salt
    2 tablespoons caraway seed
       About 3½ cups all-purpose flour,
          unsifted
    2 cups dark rye flour, unsifted
    2 tablespoons yellow cornmeal

Pour sugar into a heavy 10-inch frying pan. Place over medium-high heat until sugar is melted; stir constantly with a fork. Continue to cook until sugar smokes and is very dark (about 2½ minutes). When all the sugar is black, add boiling water and continue to cook, stirring constantly, until all sugar is dissolved and liquid is reduced to ½ cup. Remove from heat and stir in shortening; let cool.

In a large bowl, dissolve yeast in water. Add cooled caramel liquid, cocoa, salt, caraway seed, and 2 cups of the all-purpose flour. Beat until smooth. Add rye flour and beat for at least 5 minutes. Work in 1 more cup all-purpose flour to make a stiff dough.

Turn dough out onto a floured board, cover, and let rest for 10 minutes. Then knead until dough is elastic

and just tacky to the touch (10 to 20 minutes), adding flour as needed to prevent sticking.

Turn dough over in a greased bowl; cover and let rise in a warm place until doubled (about 1 hour). Punch down dough, knead briefly on a lightly floured board to release air, and divide in half. Shape each half into a ball, flatten slightly, and place on a baking sheet (or place both loaves 3 to 4 inches apart on a single larger sheet). Cover and let rise until almost doubled (about 1 hour and 15 minutes).

Bake in a 375° oven for 35 minutes or until bread sounds hollow when tapped. Let cool on rack. Makes 2 loaves.

A traditional gesture of welcome in Russia is to offer visitors a loaf of dark bread and a pile of salt. The guest breaks off a chunk of bread, dips it in the salt, and eats it.

European Sour Bread

Flat beer—that's the surprising ingredient used by European bakers to create a distinctive tart flavor in breads.

This European-style dark bread combines the beer with molasses, wheat germ, bran, and whole grain flours. The result is a wholesome, sour-flavored bread with a moist, chewy texture.

    2 cups flat beer
       About ⅔ cup yellow cornmeal
    2 tablespoons butter or margarine
    2 teaspoons salt
    ½ cup *each* dark molasses and warm water
          (about 110°)
    2 packages active dry yeast
    1 tablespoon sugar
    ½ cup *each* wheat germ and whole bran
          cereal
    2 cups graham flour or whole wheat flour,
          unsifted
    1 cup gluten flour or all-purpose flour,
          unsifted
       About 3½ cups all-purpose flour,
          unsifted
    1 egg yolk mixed with 1 tablespoon water

In a pan over medium heat, heat beer to steaming. Remove from heat and gradually stir in ½ cup of the cornmeal, the butter, salt, and molasses; set aside to cool to lukewarm.

Meanwhile, in a large bowl, combine water, yeast, and sugar; let stand until bubbly (about 15 minutes).

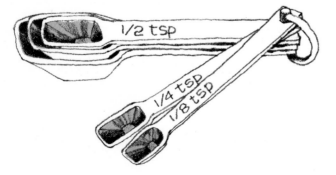

Gradually beat in cooled beer mixture, wheat germ, bran, graham flour, and gluten flour. Gradually stir in enough of the all-purpose flour (about 3 cups) to make a stiff dough. Turn dough out onto a board sprinkled with about ¼ cup of the remaining all-purpose flour. Knead until smooth and satiny (10 to 20 minutes), adding flour as needed to prevent sticking.

Turn dough over in greased bowl; cover and let rise in a warm place until doubled (about 1 hour). Punch dough down, cover, and let rise again until doubled (about 45 minutes).

Sprinkle 2 greased baking sheets (or 1 larger sheet) evenly with about 2 tablespoons cornmeal. Punch dough down, knead briefly on a lightly floured board to release air, and divide in half. Shape each half into a slightly flattened 8-inch round; place on a baking sheet (or place both loaves 3 to 4 inches apart on a single larger sheet). Cover and let rise until almost doubled (about 40 minutes).

Using a razor blade or a sharp floured knife, make ½-inch-deep slashes on top of loaves, forming a tic-tac-toe design; brush tops and sides with egg yolk mixture. Bake in a 375° oven for 40 minutes or until bread is well browned and sounds hollow when tapped. Let cool on rack. Makes 2 round loaves.

Two-tone Twisted Loaf

In a single slice of this novel loaf, you get a taste of two quite different kinds of bread—light oatmeal and dark pumpernickel. Because the loaf is twisted, each slice differs from the next in pattern and proportion of light and dark bread.

The two recipes that follow were developed especially for this twisted loaf—the two doughs must have the same amount of yeast in proportion to flour so they will both rise in the same time.

(Continued on page 23)

What Shape Shall I Bake?

The standard oblong is a perfectly serviceable shape for toast or sandwich loaves—most of the time. But, for an occasional change of pace, here are a few alternatives to try when the recipe reads "divide the dough and shape ... "

Free-form loaves: Rounds and ovals are easy to shape because the dough tends to be round anyway. They keep their shape during rising and baking best if the dough is just a bit stiffer than usual. After dividing the dough, lightly knead and pat it into a ball. Gently pull around the rim to flatten the ball slightly and smooth its top; pinch underneath to seal any crevices. To form an oval, just roll with your hands and gently pull both ends of the ball to elongate it slightly.

Let free-form loaves rise, covered, on greased baking sheets. When ready to bake, if the loaves are rather high, slash them with a razor blade or sharp floured knife, making ½-inch-deep cuts. Traditional patterns include three evenly spaced parallel cuts, a cross, and a crisscross lattice. Besides making the loaf attractive, the slashes allow steam to escape during baking, preventing the crust from cracking.

Long loaves: Shape them by rolling the dough back and forth with your hands, gently pulling it to form a smooth rope. Don't make the loaves too long, though, or they may outgrow the baking sheet as they rise. Cover and let rise.

Rolled-up shapes: These are particularly attractive when wrapped around a filling, jelly-roll fashion; even without a filling, some people like this method for shaping a standard loaf. Roll the dough into a smooth rectangle of the size specified in the recipe (or roll until the two short sides of the rectangle almost equal the length of your loaf pan). Spread the filling over the dough; then, starting at one narrow end, roll dough up tightly into a log, pinching the edges to seal. Pull the ends underneath, place seam side down in a greased loaf pan, cover, and let rise.

Braids: Divide the dough for one loaf into three or four equal portions. Shape each into a smooth rope as directed for long loaves. Lay the ropes side by side on a greased baking sheet; pinch them together at one end. Working from right to left, lay the first rope over the next one and under the third (and over the fourth, if using four strands). Repeat, always starting at the right, until the braid is complete. Pinch the ends to seal and tuck underneath. Cover and let rise.

Unusual pans: Virtually any baking pan (and even clay flower pots or recycled cans) will take the place of a standard loaf pan. Just be sure that the volume of the alternative container is about equal to that of the pan suggested in the recipe—compare by measuring how much water it takes to fill them. For a loaf with an attractively rounded top, the dough should generally fill about two thirds of whatever container you bake it in.

. . . Two-tone Twisted Loaf (cont'd.)

Pumpernickel Bread

   2 packages active dry yeast
 ½ cup warm water (about 110°)
   2 cups warm milk (about 110°)
   2 tablespoons *each* dark molasses and
        Postum
   1 tablespoon caraway seed
   2 teaspoons salt
3½ cups all-purpose flour, unsifted
   1 cup whole bran cereal
2½ cups rye flour, unsifted

In a large bowl, dissolve yeast in water. Add milk, molasses, Postum, caraway seed, salt, and 2 cups of the all-purpose flour; beat well to blend. Then beat in bran cereal and enough of the remaining all-purpose flour to form a soft dough.

Turn out onto a board coated with rye flour. Gradually knead in all the rye flour, making a stiff dough. Then knead until smooth and elastic (10 to 20 minutes).

Turn dough over in a greased bowl; cover and let stand at room temperature while you prepare Oatmeal Bread (recipe follows); then let rise in a warm place until doubled (about 1 hour). Punch dough down and knead briefly on a lightly floured board to release air. Dough is now ready to shape with Oatmeal Bread.

Oatmeal Bread

   2 packages active dry yeast
 ½ cup warm water (about 110°)
   3 cups quick-cooking rolled oats
   2 tablespoons sugar
   2 teaspoons salt
   2 cups warm milk (about 110°)
4¼ cups all-purpose flour, unsifted
   1 egg white beaten with 1 tablespoon water

In a large bowl, dissolve yeast in water. Whirl rolled oats in blender until powdery (you should have 2¼ cups). To yeast mixture, add sugar, salt, milk, and 2 cups of the flour; beat well to blend. Then beat in enough of the remaining flour to make a soft dough. Turn out onto a board coated with rolled oats.

Gradually knead in all the rolled oats, making a stiff dough. Then knead until smooth and elastic (10 to 20 minutes).

Turn dough over in a greased bowl; cover and let rise in a warm place until doubled (about 1 hour). Punch dough down, and knead briefly on a lightly floured board to release air. Dough is now ready to shape with Pumpernickel Bread (preceding recipe).

To shape, divide both doughs in half; set aside half of each dough and cover with a slightly damp cloth. Roll oatmeal dough into an even strand about 16 inches long. Roll pumpernickel dough to same length. Place strands parallel on a lightly greased baking sheet and twist them together as shown below, twisting without stretching. Make twists even and parallel. Brush dough lightly with egg white-water mixture. On another baking sheet, prepare and twist remaining 2 pieces of dough in same way. Let rise in a warm place until puffy (about 30 minutes).

Bake in a 350° oven for 30 minutes or until loaves are lightly browned and sound hollow when tapped. Let cool on rack. Makes 2 large loaves.

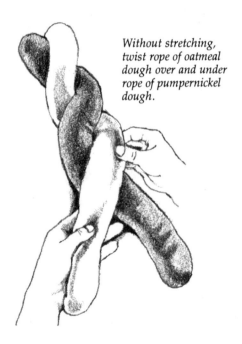

Without stretching, twist rope of oatmeal dough over and under rope of pumpernickel dough.

Onion Boards

These puffy-rimmed, rectangular breads have a bagel-like chewy texture and an authoritative flavor from toasted onion bits that are liberally strewn on their flat tops. When they're served warm, their aroma is irresistible.

Served whole or broken apart, onion boards are good companions to a soup or salad for a light, satisfying meal.

(Continued on next page)

> 1 **package active dry yeast**
> 2 **cups warm water (about 110°)**
> 2 **tablespoons sugar**
> 2 **teaspoons salt**
> 5½ **to 6 cups all-purpose flour, unsifted**
> ¾ **cup instant minced onion**
> **Water**
> 1 **egg yolk beaten with 1 tablespoon water**

In a large bowl, dissolve yeast in warm water. Stir in sugar, salt, and about 2 cups of the flour. Beat in 2 to 3 cups more flour to make a stiff dough. Turn out onto a floured board; knead until smooth and satiny (5 to 20 minutes), adding flour as needed to prevent sticking. Turn dough over in a greased bowl; cover and let rise in a warm place until doubled (about 1½ hours).

Punch dough down; knead briefly on a lightly floured board to release air. Divide into 6 equal parts, cover lightly, and let rest for 10 minutes. Soak onion in enough water to cover for 5 to 10 minutes; then squeeze out excess moisture.

On a lightly floured board, roll and stretch each portion of dough into a rectangle about 7 by 11 inches; edges should be slightly raised. Lightly brush with egg yolk and water mixture and then transfer to a lightly greased baking sheet. Distribute onion evenly over top.

Bake 1 or 2 at a time in a 375° oven for 20 to 25 minutes or until golden brown; let cool on racks. Unbaked boards can stand, uncovered, as necessary, until placed in oven. Makes 6 boards.

Quick Potato Bread

This streamlined version of an old European recipe for potato bread makes two tender, even-textured loaves. Though the potato contributes no readily detectable flavor, it does give a pleasant aroma and moistness to the bread and helps to keep it fresh-tasting for several days.

An electric mixer lets you take advantage of a short-cut mixing method. Instead of dissolving the yeast in water, you combine it with some of the flour and the other dry ingredients, add the potatoes and liquid, then beat well. Once most of the flour has been beaten into the mixture, little kneading is required to develop a smooth, elastic dough that is easy to handle.

> 1 **package active dry yeast**
> 4 **to 4½ cups all-purpose flour, unsifted**
> ¼ **cup sugar**
> 2 **teaspoons salt**
> **Instant mashed potatoes (amount for 2 servings)**
> ¾ **cup milk**
> ¼ **cup butter or margarine, melted**
> 2 **eggs**

In large bowl of an electric mixer, stir together yeast, 1½ cups of the flour, sugar, and salt. In a pan, prepare 2 servings of instant mashed potatoes according to package directions, using amounts of water, milk, butter, and salt called for on package. Then stir in milk, melted butter, and eggs; stir until well blended.

Add potato mixture to dry ingredients and beat for 2 minutes at medium speed, scraping bowl occasionally. Add 1 more cup of the flour and beat at medium speed for 2 minutes longer. With a spoon, stir in 1 more cup of the flour to form a stiff dough. Turn dough out onto a floured board; knead until smooth and satiny (5 to 20 minutes), adding flour as needed to prevent sticking.

Turn dough over in a greased bowl; cover and let rise in a warm place until doubled (1½ to 2 hours). Punch dough down, knead briefly to release air, and shape into 2 loaves. Place each in a well-greased 9 by 5-inch loaf pan. Cover and let rise in a warm place until almost doubled (about 45 minutes).

Bake in a 350° oven for 35 minutes or until loaves are well browned and sound hollow when tapped. Turn out on a rack to cool. Makes 2 loaves.

Rosemary Raisin Bread

This plump Italian raisin bread is seasoned with rosemary and olive oil. It is delicious warm with butter for brunch or served with salads or soups for lunch. You can make it ahead and reheat before serving, or slice and toast.

1 package active dry yeast
¼ cup warm water (about 110°)
½ cup milk
3 tablespoons sugar
1 teaspoon *each* salt and dry rosemary
2 eggs
¼ cup olive oil
3 to 3½ cups all-purpose flour, unsifted
½ cup raisins
  Olive oil
1 tablespoon cold water

In a large bowl, dissolve yeast in warm water. In a pan, combine milk, sugar, salt, and rosemary; heat until warm (about 110°). Beat in 1 whole egg, 1 egg white (reserve yolk of second egg for glaze), and the ¼ cup olive oil; add to dissolved yeast. Gradually beat in about 2½ cups of the flour to make a stiff dough. Turn out onto a well-floured board and knead until smooth and satiny (10 to 20 minutes), adding flour as needed to prevent sticking. Flatten dough, top with raisins, and knead lightly to work them into dough (some pop out, but just push them back in).

Turn dough over in bowl oiled with olive oil. Cover and let rise in a warm place until doubled (1 to 1½ hours).

Punch dough down; knead briefly on a lightly floured board to release air. Place on an olive-oil-coated baking sheet and pat into a flat round, about 8½ inches in diameter. Brush generously with olive oil, cover, and let rise in a warm place until puffy (about 30 minutes).

With a razor blade or sharp floured knife, slash a cross in top of loaf. Beat reserved egg yolk with the 1 tablespoon cold water and brush over loaf. Bake in a 350° oven for about 35 minutes or until loaf is browned and sounds hollow when tapped. Cool on a rack. Makes 1 loaf.

Carrot Wheat Bread

Those who want their bread to have the heft and flavor of whole grains will delight in this hearty loaf. It combines the nutlike quality of stone-ground whole wheat flour with the mild sweetness of honey. And the raisins and carrot make the bread pleasingly moist and interesting.

1 package active dry yeast
⅓ cup warm water (about 110°)
2 cups milk, at room temperature
5 tablespoons butter or margarine, melted
2 teaspoons salt
½ cup honey
6 to 6½ cups stone-ground whole wheat
    flour, unsifted
1 cup shredded carrot
1 cup raisins

In a large bowl, dissolve yeast in water. Add milk, 3 tablespoons of the butter, salt, and honey. Gradually beat in 5 cups of the flour to make a soft dough; stir in carrot and raisins. Turn dough out onto well-floured board (use about ¾ cup); knead until smooth and elastic (10 to 20 minutes), adding flour as needed to prevent sticking.

Turn dough over in a greased bowl; cover and let rise in a warm place until doubled (about 3 hours). Punch dough down, knead briefly on a lightly floured board to release air, and divide in half. Shape each into a smooth, round loaf. Place each loaf on a greased baking sheet. Cover and let rise until almost doubled (about 1 hour).

Brush tops with remaining 2 tablespoons butter. Bake in a 350° oven for about 30 minutes or until loaves are browned and sound hollow when tapped. Let cool on racks. Makes 2 loaves.

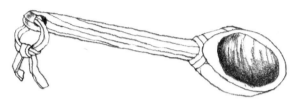

Little Breads

Party Bread Sticks

This recipe makes dramatically long bread sticks—16 or 20 inches—to add spectacle to a simple spaghetti dinner. Or you can make 12-inch sticks to serve with sweet butter as a delicious accompaniment to apéritif wines. *(Photograph on page 27.)*

The length of the sticks is limited only by the dimensions of your oven (measure your freezer shelf, too, if you plan to freeze them). You can bake them on a foil-topped oven rack or on a large rimless baking sheet. You might put two sheets together end to end, wrapping them around the middle with foil; or use the bottom of a large roasting pan, inverted. For good heat circulation in the oven, always allow at least an inch on all sides of the foil or pan.

4 to 4½ cups all-purpose flour, unsifted
1 tablespoon sugar
1 teaspoon salt
2 packages active dry yeast
¼ cup olive oil or salad oil
1¼ cups hot water (120° to 130°)
1 egg white beaten with 1 tablespoon water
  Coarse salt, toasted sesame seed, or
    poppy seed (optional)

In the large bowl of an electric mixer stir together 1 cup of the flour, the sugar, salt, and yeast. Add oil, then gradually stir in hot water. Beat at medium speed for 2 minutes. Add ½ cup more flour and beat at high speed for 2 minutes. Stir in 1½ to 2 cups of the remaining flour with your mixer (if it's a heavy-duty model) or a wooden spoon to make a soft dough.

Turn dough out onto a well-floured board and, with well-floured hands, work it into a smooth ball. With a sharp knife, cut into 20 equal pieces for 16-inch sticks—or 16 pieces for 20-inch sticks, depending on size of pan and oven. Roll each piece of dough into a rope that is 16 or 20 inches long. Arrange about 1 inch apart on oiled baking sheets or oiled foil placed on oven racks, rolling to grease all sides of dough.

At this point you may wish to cover tightly with clear plastic wrap and freeze until solid. Then transfer to plastic bags and store in freezer up to 4 weeks. Remove frozen sticks from freezer about 30 minutes before you plan to bake them. Arrange frozen bread sticks about 1 inch apart on ungreased baking sheets or foil-topped oven racks; cover and let stand at room temperature until fully thawed (about 15 minutes).

Set bread sticks (thaw first, if frozen) in a warm place, cover, and let rise until puffy (about 15 minutes). With a soft brush, paint each stick with egg white-water mixture. Sprinkle lightly with coarse salt or either of the seeds, or leave plain, if you prefer. Bake in a 375° oven for about 15 to 20 minutes or until lightly browned all over. Makes 16 to 20 extra-large bread sticks.

For appetizer bread sticks, divide dough into 40 equal pieces and roll each to about 12 inches long. Freeze or bake as directed for larger sticks, on oiled baking sheets or oiled foil placed on oven racks. Bake in a 375° oven for 10 to 15 minutes or until golden brown.

Cottage Cheese Pan Rolls

Cottage cheese makes these speedy rolls moist and light. For a flavor variation, you might try adding 2 teaspoons dill weed with the cottage cheese.

    1 package active dry yeast
    ½ cup warm water (about 110°)
    1 cup large curd cottage cheese
    1 egg
    2 teaspoons baking powder
    ¼ teaspoon soda
    1 teaspoon salt
    1 tablespoon sugar
    3½ to 4 cups all-purpose flour, unsifted
    2 tablespoons firm butter or margarine

In a small bowl, dissolve yeast in water. Combine cottage cheese and egg in a blender; whirl until smooth.

In a large bowl, stir together baking powder, soda, salt, sugar, and 3¼ cups of the flour. Work butter into flour mixture with your fingers until no large particles remain. Stir in cheese mixture and yeast.

Wine, candlelight, and something to nibble—crisp, seed-studded Party Bread Sticks (page 25).

Turn dough out onto a floured board and knead until smooth and satiny (5 to 20 minutes), adding flour as needed to prevent sticking. Turn dough over in a greased bowl; cover and let rise until doubled (about 30 minutes). Punch dough down. Divide into 18 equal pieces. Roll each into a ball and arrange in 2 greased 8-inch round baking pans. Cover and let stand for 10 minutes.

Bake in a 350° oven for about 25 minutes or until golden. Cool on racks. Makes 1½ dozen.

Salt Snacks

These savory tidbits, crunchy with coarse salt and caraway seed, make a delicious afternoon or late evening snack. Or try them as an intriguing little bread to go with soup.

    2 packages active dry yeast
    1 cup warm water (about 110°)
    1 small can (about 5 oz.) evaporated milk
    ¼ cup sugar
    2 teaspoons salt
    3 tablespoons salad oil
    3½ to 4 cups all-purpose flour, unsifted
    1 egg white, lightly beaten
    2 tablespoons *each* coarse salt and caraway seed

In a large bowl, dissolve yeast in water. Stir in milk, sugar, salt, and oil. Beat in 2 cups of the flour until smooth; then beat in about 1 cup of the remaining flour to make a soft dough. Turn dough out onto a floured board; knead until smooth and satiny (10 to 20 minutes). Turn dough over in a greased bowl; cover and let rise until doubled (about 1 hour).

Punch dough down; knead briefly on a lightly floured board to release air. Divide dough into 4 equal portions; let rest 10 minutes. Shape each portion into a ball, then roll out into a 10-inch circle and cut each circle into 8 wedges. Beginning at wide end, roll up each wedge tightly. Place on greased baking sheets with points down; brush with egg white, then sprinkle with coarse salt and caraway seed. Let rise until puffy (about 30 minutes).

Bake in a 400° oven for 15 minutes or until browned. Makes 32 salt snacks.

Whole Wheat Roll Menagerie

With this yeast dough that models like clay and stays tender through shaping and reshaping, you can create a menagerie of dinner roll animals. Or try other bread sculptures—fruits, vegetables, or people, if you like (see page 61). Keep in mind that simple, bold shapes work best. Thin or small pieces of dough get too brown in the oven before the roll is completely baked. You can also use seeds, nuts, or whole cloves for decoration.

> 1 package active dry yeast
> 1 cup warm water (about 110°)
> 2 tablespoons molasses
> 1 tablespoon salad oil
> 1 teaspoon salt
> ¼ cup wheat germ
> 1¾ cups whole wheat flour, unsifted
> 1¼ to 1½ cups all-purpose flour, unsifted
> 1 egg yolk mixed with 2 teaspoons water

In a large bowl, dissolve yeast in water. Add molasses, oil, salt, wheat germ, and whole wheat flour. Beat well to blend. Gradually beat in about 1 cup of the all-purpose flour to make a stiff dough.

Turn dough out onto floured board; knead until smooth and satiny (5 to 20 minutes), adding flour as needed to prevent sticking. Turn dough over in a greased bowl; cover and let rise in a warm place until doubled (about 1½ hours).

Punch dough down, knead briefly to release air, then divide into 7 pieces. Form each on a very lightly floured board, creating animal shapes (see examples below); keep unshaped dough lightly covered.

Place rolls about 2 inches apart on well-greased baking sheets. Cover lightly and let rise in a warm place until puffy (about 25 to 30 minutes). It's easier if you let the first 2 or 3 rolls rise while you shape the others; then bake in batches. Before baking, brush each roll lightly with the yolk-water mixture.

Bake in a 400° oven for about 15 to 20 minutes or until nicely browned. Cool on racks. Makes 7 rolls.

Onion-Herb Hot Dog Buns

Using this refrigerator dough, you can make fresh buns to fit your favorite long or short frankfurters—doing most of the preparation in advance.

> 2 packages active dry yeast
> 2 cups warm water (about 110°)
> ⅓ cup *each* sugar and nonfat dry milk
> ⅓ cup butter, margarine, or shortening, at room temperature
> 1 egg
> 2½ teaspoons salt
> 1½ teaspoons caraway seed
> 2 tablespoons instant toasted onion
> ½ teaspoon dry basil or oregano leaves
> ¼ teaspoon garlic powder
> 6½ to 7 cups all-purpose flour, unsifted
> Butter or margarine, melted

In a large bowl, dissolve yeast in water. Stir in sugar, nonfat dry milk, butter, egg, salt, caraway seed, toasted onion, basil and garlic powder. Beat in about 6 cups of the flour to make a soft dough. Turn dough out onto a floured board; knead until smooth (about 5 minutes—dough will be a little sticky). Turn dough over in a greased bowl, cover with clear plastic wrap, and refrigerate for 24 hours or as long as 4 days.

To shape into buns, punch dough down and turn out on an unfloured board. For long frankfurters (about 9 inches long), divide dough into 16 equal pieces. For regular frankfurters (about 6 inches long), divide dough into 24 equal pieces. Roll each piece of dough into a smooth 9-inch-long rope for long buns or a 6-inch-long rope for regular-size buns. Place about 2 inches apart on lightly greased baking sheets and flatten slightly. Cover and let rise in a warm place until almost doubled (1 to 1¼ hours).

Brush each bun with melted butter and bake in a 400° oven for about 10 to 12 minutes or until golden brown. Let cool on wire racks. Package airtight to store or freeze. Use a serrated knife to cut buns in half lengthwise. Makes 16 long or 24 regular-size buns.

Whole Wheat Roll Menagerie

Your menagerie might include a butterfly, a turtle, and a baby octopus (recipe appears above left).

Gemini Rolls

These whole wheat rolls were named after the astrological Gemini twins because they have two identical sides. They are shaped to fit neatly around the split halves of a big, juicy sausage for hearty supper sandwiches. For a party, you might offer them with a selection of heat-and-serve garlic frankfurters, Polish sausages, bratwurst, and old-fashioned frankfurters.

1 package active dry yeast
2¼ cups warm water (about 110°)
2 tablespoons firmly packed brown sugar
2 teaspoons salt
1 tablespoon salad oil
3 cups whole wheat flour, unsifted
3 to 3½ cups all-purpose flour, unsifted
1 teaspoon cornstarch dissolved in ½ cup water

In a large bowl, dissolve yeast in water. Stir in brown sugar, salt, and oil; then beat in 1½ cups *each* of the whole wheat and all-purpose flours.

Gradually beat in remaining 1½ cups whole wheat flour and 1 cup of the all-purpose flour to make a stiff dough. Turn dough out onto a floured board; knead until smooth and elastic (10 to 20 minutes), adding flour as needed to prevent sticking. Turn dough over in a greased bowl; cover and let rise in a warm place until doubled (about 1½ hours).

Punch dough down, knead briefly on a lightly floured board to release air, then divide in half. Let dough rest, lightly covered, for 10 to 15 minutes. On a lightly floured board, roll out half of the dough at a time into a 9 by 19-inch rectangle. With a sharp knife, cut across dough, making 6 strips, each 3 by 9 inches.

As shown below, shape each roll by grasping corners at 1 end of a strip and gently stretching to 5 to 6 inches. Stretch gently as you roll up toward center. Repeat, rolling other end to center. Turn over and place rolls about 2 inches apart on greased baking sheets. Cover and let rise until almost doubled (about 45 minutes).

Meanwhile, heat cornstarch and water to boiling, stirring; cool slightly. With a razor blade or sharp floured knife, cut 3 slashes about ¼ inch deep in top of each roll; brush all over with cornstarch mixture. Bake in a 400° oven for about 20 to 25 minutes or until well browned. Makes 12.

How to shape Gemini Rolls

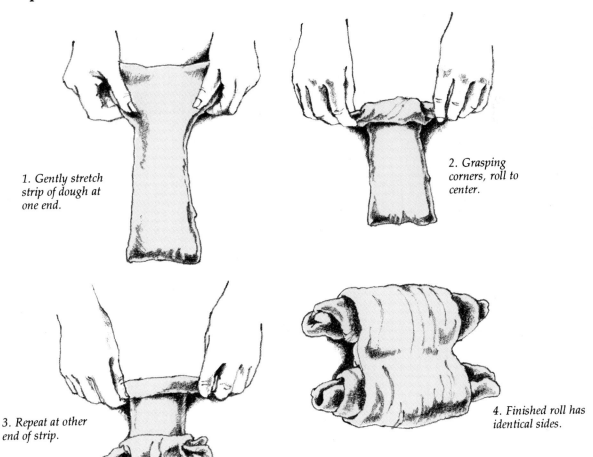

1. Gently stretch strip of dough at one end.

2. Grasping corners, roll to center.

3. Repeat at other end of strip.

4. Finished roll has identical sides.

Whole Wheat Onion Buns

Toasted onion flecks and rich wheaty flavor distinguish these crusty sandwich buns. Served warm from the oven or split, buttered, and toasted, they complement such savory enclosures as broiled hamburgers and thinly sliced roasted or barbecued beef, ham, chicken, or turkey.

The yeast dough goes together quickly, thanks to this simplified technique: instead of first dissolving the yeast in water, you blend it with some of the dry ingredients, add hot water from the tap, then beat it with an electric mixer. Only very brief kneading of the dough is required.

3 tablespoons butter or margarine
¾ cup finely chopped onion
2½ to 3 cups all-purpose flour, unsifted
3 cups whole wheat flour, unsifted
3 tablespoons sugar
1½ teaspoons salt
2 packages active dry yeast
2 cups hot tap water

In a small frying pan, melt butter; add onion and sauté until golden (5 to 7 minutes). Set aside.

In large bowl of an electric mixer, stir together 1 cup of the all-purpose flour, 1 cup of the whole wheat flour, sugar, salt, and yeast. Measure and set aside about 2 tablespoons onion-butter; then mix remaining onion-butter into yeast mixture. Pour in hot water; beat at low speed for 2 minutes.

Add 1 more cup whole wheat flour and beat at high speed for 2 minutes. Stir in remaining 1 cup whole wheat flour and enough of the all-purpose flour (about 1 cup) to make a soft dough. Sprinkle about ⅓ cup of the remaining all-purpose flour on a board; turn dough out and knead until smooth (about 5 minutes), adding flour as needed to prevent sticking. Turn dough over in a greased bowl; cover and let rise in a warm place until doubled (about 1 hour).

Punch dough down, divide into 20 equal pieces, and roll each into a ball; place balls about 4 inches apart on greased baking sheets. With greased fingers, flatten each into about a 4-inch circle. Spread about ¼ teaspoon reserved onion-butter on top of each circle. Cover and let rise until almost doubled (about 50 minutes).

Bake in a 375° oven for 20 to 25 minutes or until brown. Let cool on racks. Makes 20 rolls.

Raised Buttermilk Biscuits

This cross between a biscuit and a roll has some of the characteristics of each. The crust is tender, with a delicate and even texture. Because they need to rise only once, you can start these rolls in the late afternoon and serve them freshly baked for dinner.

1 package active dry yeast
1 tablespoon sugar
2 tablespoons warm water (about 110°)
2½ cups all-purpose flour, unsifted
1 teaspoon *each* baking powder and salt
2 tablespoons firm butter or margarine
⅔ cup buttermilk
Melted butter

In a small bowl, combine yeast, sugar, and water; let stand until bubbly (about 15 minutes). In a large bowl, stir together 2 cups of the flour, baking powder, and salt until well mixed. With a pastry cutter or 2 knives, cut in firm butter or margarine to fine crumb stage, as you would for ordinary biscuits. Beat in yeast mixture and buttermilk to make a moderately stiff dough.

Knead lightly for a few seconds; on a floured board, roll to ½-inch thickness. Cut dough with a 2-inch floured biscuit cutter. Arrange biscuits in a greased baking pan so they barely touch each other; prick tops in several places with a fork and brush with melted butter. Let rise in a warm place until almost doubled (30 to 40 minutes).

Bake in a 425° oven for 10 to 15 minutes or until golden. Makes about 1 dozen.

Buttery Pan Rolls

Light, fluffy, and delicious, these yeast batter rolls require no kneading—and they rise quickly. Served hot, right in the baking pan, they make the simplest meal a sensation.

2 packages active dry yeast
½ cup warm water (about 110°)
4½ cups all-purpose flour, unsifted
¼ cup sugar
1 teaspoon salt
1 cup plus 2 tablespoons butter or margarine, melted and cooled
1 egg
1 cup warm milk (about 110°)

In a large bowl, dissolve yeast in water; let stand until bubbly (about 15 minutes). Stir together 2 cups of the flour, the sugar, and salt until well mixed. Add 6 tablespoons of the melted butter, the egg, yeast mixture, and milk; beat for about 5 minutes to blend well. Gradually beat in remaining 2½ cups flour. Cover bowl and let batter rise in a warm place until doubled (about 45 minutes).

Pour half of the remaining melted butter into a 9 by 13-inch baking pan, tilting pan to coat bottom. Beat down batter and drop by spoonfuls into buttered pan, making about 15 rolls. Drizzle remaining melted butter over dough. Cover lightly and let rise in a warm place until almost doubled (about 30 minutes).

Bake in a 425° oven for 12 to 17 minutes or until lightly browned. Serve hot. Makes about 15 rolls.

To bake in muffin cups, make batter as directed, but instead of buttering a large pan, spoon about 1 teaspoon melted butter into each muffin cup. Fill cups about half full; let batter rise until almost doubled. Bake as above.

Whole Wheat Biscuit Buns

Crunchy seeds and wheat germ give these whole-some little breads a nutty flavor and robust texture. Serve them warm or split and toasted, spread with butter, jam, or peanut butter.

- **2 packages active dry yeast**
- **2 cups warm water (about 110°)**
- **½ cup soy oil or salad oil**
- **¼ cup *each* molasses and honey**
- **1 tablespoon salt**
- **¼ cup *each* sesame seed, hulled sunflower seeds, and wheat germ**
- **6½ to 7 cups whole wheat flour, unsifted**

In a large bowl, dissolve yeast in ½ cup of the water. Add oil, molasses, honey, salt, sesame seed, sunflower seeds, wheat germ, and 4 cups of the flour. Beat to blend well. Stir in remaining 1½ cups water. Beat in about 2 more cups flour to form a stiff dough. Turn dough out onto a floured board; knead until smooth and elastic (10 to 20 minutes), adding flour as needed to prevent sticking. Turn dough over in a greased bowl; cover and let rise in a warm place until doubled (about 1½ hours).

Punch dough down. On a lightly floured board, knead briefly to release air, then roll dough into a rectangle ½ inch thick on a floured board. Cut with a floured 2-inch biscuit cutter. Place about 1 inch apart on greased baking sheets; cover and let rise until very puffy (about 40 minutes).

Bake in a 375° oven for 20 minutes or until golden. Let cool on racks. Makes about 4 dozen.

An old Slavic proverb: "Without bread, even a palace would be sad, but with it a pine tree is paradise."

Pumpkin Pan Rolls

A generous amount of spice enhances these fine-textured yeast rolls. Try them as a companion to a hearty Halloween stew or casserole—or for an un-usual bread with your Thanksgiving feast.

- **1 package active dry yeast**
- **1 cup warm water (about 110°)**
- **½ cup sugar**
- **3 tablespoons butter or margarine, melted**
- **1 teaspoon salt**
- **½ cup nonfat dry milk**
- **1 cup canned pumpkin**
- **1½ teaspoons ground cinnamon**
- **¾ teaspoon *each* ground cloves, nutmeg, and ginger**
- **4½ to 5 cups all-purpose flour, unsifted**

In a large bowl, dissolve yeast in water. Add sugar, butter, salt, dry milk, pumpkin, cinnamon, cloves, nutmeg, and ginger. Beat well to blend; then gradu-ally beat in about 4 cups of the flour to make a stiff dough. Turn dough out onto a floured board; knead until smooth (15 to 20 minutes), adding flour as needed to prevent sticking.

Turn dough over in a greased bowl; cover and let rise in a warm place until doubled (1½ to 2 hours). Punch dough down; knead briefly on a lightly floured board to release air. Divide dough into 32 equal pieces. Shape each into a smooth ball; place balls in 2 greased 9-inch round baking pans. Cover and let rise until almost doubled (about 1 hour).

Bake in a 375° oven for 25 minutes or until browned. Cool on racks. Makes 32 rolls.

Crusty Water Rolls

These crusty glazed rolls have a soft, moist interior and a crunchy cornmeal bottom crust. Sharing the oven with a shallow pan of hot water is the secret of their special crust.

- **1 cup warm water (about 110°)**
- **1 tablespoon sugar**
- **1½ teaspoons salt**
- **1 package active dry yeast**
- **3½ to 4 cups all-purpose flour, unsifted**
- **2 tablespoons salad oil**
- **2 egg whites**
- **Cornmeal**
- **1 egg yolk beaten with 1 tablespoon water**

In a large bowl, combine water, sugar, salt, and yeast; let stand until bubbly (about 15 minutes). Then add 1 cup of the flour and the oil; beat until smooth. Beat egg whites until stiff but not dry; fold into batter. Gradually beat in about 2 cups of the remaining flour to make a stiff dough. Turn dough out onto a floured board; knead until smooth and satiny (5 to 20 minutes), adding flour as needed to prevent sticking.

Turn dough over in a greased bowl. Cover and let rise in a warm place until doubled (about 1 hour). Punch dough down, cover, and let rise 15 minutes longer. Punch dough down again, knead briefly on a lightly floured board to release air, and divide into 18 pieces. Shape each piece into a ball; dip bottoms in cornmeal. Place balls, about 1½ inches apart, on a greased baking sheet. Cover and let rise until almost doubled (about 50 minutes).

Brush rolls with egg yolk mixture. Place a shallow pan of hot water on lowest oven rack. Bake rolls in a 400° oven just above pan of water for 15 to 20 minutes or until richly browned. Cool on racks. Makes 1½ dozen rolls.

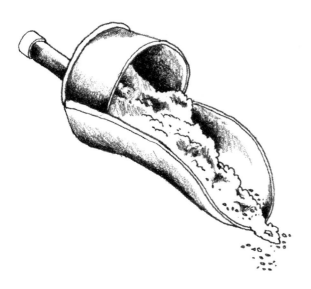

Traditional Breads

Sally Lunn

Sally Lunn is said to have been an English pastry cook and baker who made and served a light, eggy yeast cake at her refreshment house in the town of Bath around 1680. Her specialty—a cross between a cake and a batter bread—soon came to be known by her name.

- 1 package active dry yeast
- ½ cup warm water (about 110°)
- 1 cup milk
- ½ cup (¼ lb.) butter or margarine
- ⅓ cup sugar
- 1 teaspoon salt
- 3 eggs
- 5½ to 6 cups all-purpose flour, unsifted

In a large bowl, dissolve yeast in water. In a pan, heat milk with butter (cut into small pieces), sugar, and salt to about 110° (butter need not melt completely). Add to dissolved yeast; stir in eggs and 3 cups of the flour; beat until smooth.

Beat in enough of the remaining flour (about 2½ to 3 cups) to make dough stiff but too sticky to knead. Cover; let rise in a warm place until doubled (about 1½ hours). Stir dough down and turn into a well-buttered 10-inch tube pan with removable bottom. Push and punch dough to cover pan bottom evenly. Cover and let rise in a warm place until level with pan top (about 1 hour).

Bake in a 375° oven for about 35 minutes or until well browned. Run a long spatula around pan sides; lift out tube and bread. Loosen bottom of bread with spatula; invert and twist tube gently to remove. Let cool standing upright on a rack. Cut in thin wedges. Makes 1 large loaf.

Crumpets

Crumpets have holes for a reason. How else, ask the British, can a generous amount of butter properly permeate each moist and springy bite?

Crumpets can probably best be described as a cross between an English muffin and a pancake. They are served warm, either freshly baked or toasted, with butter and jam, marmalade, or honey.

You'll need some kind of metal rings to contain the simple yeast batter while it bakes in a frying pan or on a griddle. You can use 3-inch flan rings or open-topped cooky cutters. Or you can do as we did—use tuna cans with the tops and bottoms removed. (*Photograph on page 30.*)

- 1 package active dry yeast
- 1 teaspoon sugar
- ¼ cup warm water (about 110°)
- ⅓ cup milk, at room temperature
- 1 egg
  About 4 tablespoons butter or margarine, melted
- 1 cup all-purpose flour, unsifted
- ½ teaspoon salt

In a large bowl, combine yeast, sugar, and water; let stand until bubbly (about 15 minutes). Blend in milk, egg, and 1 tablespoon of the butter. Add flour and salt and beat until smooth. Cover and let stand in a warm place until almost doubled (about 45 minutes).

Brush bottom of a heavy frying pan or griddle and the inside of each 3-inch ring with butter. Heat rings in pan over low heat; pour about 3 tablespoons batter into each ring. Bake for about 7 minutes or until holes appear and tops are dry. Remove rings and turn crumpets to brown other side lightly (about 2 minutes). Repeat with remaining batter.

Serve warm, or cool on a rack and toast just before serving. Makes 7 or 8 crumpets.

Baguettes

"Good morning" in France means a breakfast tray with Croissants (Traditional on page 36, Quick Butter on page 37) and Brioches (below).

In France, bread is still very much the staff of life. Many different kinds are enjoyed with different meals, but by far the most popular is the *baguette* with its shiny crust and chewy texture. You can't quite fit the typical 2-foot-long baguette in a conventional oven, but you can probably bake a loaf that's at least 18 inches long. (*Photograph on page 38.*)

Before starting your bread dough, measure the width and depth of your oven. You'll need a pan that measures at least 18 inches diagonally and that will fit in your oven with at least 1 inch free space between pan and oven walls on all four sides. You might overlap two rimless baking sheets, wrapping them around the middle with foil to hold them steady. Or consider using the bottom of a large, inverted roasting pan or rimmed baking sheet.

- 2 **cups water**
- 2 **tablespoons butter or margarine**
- 1½ **tablespoons sugar**
- 1 **tablespoon salt**
- 1 **package active dry yeast**
- 6 **to 6½ cups all-purpose flour, unsifted**
- 1 **teaspoon cornstarch dissolved in ⅔ cup water**

In a pan, combine water, butter, sugar, and salt; heat, stirring, to about 110° (butter need not melt completely). Pour into a large bowl; stir in yeast and let stand until bubbly (about 15 minutes). Beat in about 5½ cups of the flour to form a stiff dough.

Turn dough out onto a floured board; knead until smooth and satiny (5 to 20 minutes), adding flour as needed to prevent sticking. Turn dough over in a greased bowl; cover and let rise in a warm place until doubled (1 to 1½ hours). Punch dough down; divide into 3 equal pieces.

If you have only one oven, wrap 2 pieces of dough in clear plastic wrap and refrigerate. On a lightly floured board, form one piece of dough into a smooth log by gently kneading and rolling the dough back and forth until it is 10 to 12 inches long. For a smooth, well-shaped loaf, press a trench lengthwise down center of dough; then fold dough in half lengthwise along trench. With a gentle kneading motion, seal along edge by pressing against fold with heel of your hand, rolling and pushing sealed edge underneath.

With palms of your hands on center of loaf, begin rolling it back and forth rapidly, gently pulling from center to ends as you slide your hands toward ends until loaf is about 18 to 20 inches long (depending on oven size).

Place loaf diagonally across a greased baking sheet; cover and let rise in a warm place until puffy but not doubled (about 15 to 20 minutes).

In a pan, heat cornstarch and water to boiling; cool slightly. Brush entire loaf (including side of loaf resting on baking sheet) with cornstarch mixture. With a razor blade or a sharp floured knife, cut slanting slashes across loaf about ½ inch deep at 2-inch intervals down length of loaf.

Bake in a 375° oven (place oven rack just below middle of oven) for 15 minutes; then evenly brush loaf again with cornstarch mixture. Bake for 15 minutes longer and again brush with cornstarch mixture. Bake for about 10 more minutes or until loaf is golden brown and sounds hollow when tapped (35 to 40 minutes total). Cool on rack.

When you put first loaf in oven to bake, remove second piece of dough from refrigerator and shape as you did the first, placing loaf on a piece of foil to rise. It will take about 30 minutes to rise until puffy (third loaf will take slightly longer). Bake as directed. As you put second loaf in to bake, shape third piece of dough and then bake as directed.

For maximum flavor and freshness, serve bread the same day it is baked; or cool completely, wrap tightly, and freeze. To reheat, place in a 350° oven, uncovered, for about 15 minutes or until warm. Makes 3 long loaves.

Brioches, Big and Little

Eggy and rich with butter, *brioches* are truly an elegant bread. In France, brioches come in many different shapes and sizes. We offer you the two best-known: the *petite brioche* (little brioche), a roll with a fluted rim and a topknot, and the *brioche à tête* (brioche with a head), which is a grand-scale version of a petite brioche. (*Photograph on facing page.*)

- 1 **package active dry yeast**
- ½ **cup warm water (about 110°)**
- 2 **teaspoons sugar**
- 1¼ **teaspoons salt**
- 3 **eggs**
- ½ **cup (¼ lb.) butter or margarine, at room temperature**
- 3½ **to 4 cups all-purpose flour, unsifted**
- 1 **egg yolk beaten with 1 tablespoon milk**

In a large bowl, dissolve yeast in water. Stir in sugar, salt, and eggs. Cut butter or margarine into small pieces and add to liquid. Gradually beat in 3⅓ cups flour, mixing until flour is evenly moistened and dough holds together. Shape into a ball and place on a floured board. Knead until smooth and satiny (5 to 20 minutes), adding flour as needed to prevent sticking.

(Continued on page 36)

Turn dough over in a greased bowl; cover and let rise in a warm place until doubled (1 to 2 hours). Punch dough down; knead briefly on a lightly floured board to release air. Return to greased bowl; turn over to grease top. Cover with clear plastic wrap and refrigerate for 12 to 24 hours.

Knead on a lightly floured board to release air.

To make petites brioches, divide dough into 24 equal pieces. Dough is easiest to handle if kept cold, so shape a few at a time, keeping remaining pieces covered separately and refrigerated until ready to use.

Pinch off about ⅛ of each portion and set aside. Shape larger section into a smooth ball by pulling surface of dough to underside of ball; this is very important if you want to achieve a good-looking brioche. Set ball, smooth side up, in a well-buttered 3 to 4-inch petite brioche pan, fluted tart pan, or 3-inch muffin cup. Press dough down to fill pan bottom evenly. Shape small piece of dough into a teardrop that is smooth on top.

With your finger, poke a hole in center of brioche dough in pan and insert pointed end of small piece in hole, settling securely (otherwise, topknot will pop off at an angle while baking). Repeat until all brioches are shaped. If you work quickly, you can leave pans at room temperature when filled; otherwise, return filled pans, lightly covered, to refrigerator.

Cover filled pans and let stand in a warm place until almost doubled (1 to 2 hours). With a soft brush, paint tops of brioches with egg yolk-milk mixture; do not let glaze accumulate in joint of topknot.

Bake in a 425° oven for about 20 minutes or until richly browned. Remove from pans and serve warm, or let cool on racks. Makes 24.

To make brioche à tête, pinch off 1/6 of dough for a topknot. Shape both portions of dough as for a petite brioche. Place in well-buttered fluted brioche pan (9 inches across top) or 2-quart round baking pan. Following directions for petites brioches, let rise, and glaze.

Bake in a 350° oven for about 1 hour or until well browned and bread begins to pull away from sides of pan. Let stand 5 minutes; then carefully invert from pan. Serve warm, or let cool on rack. Freeze to store. Makes 1 loaf.

Traditional Croissants

The French pamper themselves in the morning with a light, elegant breakfast of *café au lait* (coffee with hot milk) and tender, flaky *croissants* (crescent rolls). These buttery little breads are a superb way to start the day (though they are delicious at any other time, too). As with any breakfast roll, you may want to make them the day before, bake them until almost done, and then finish browning them in the morning. *(Photograph on page 35.)*

1 **package active dry yeast**
¼ **cup warm water (about 110°)**
¾ **cup warm milk (about 110°)**
1 **tablespoon sugar**
½ **teaspoon salt**
3 **to 3½ cups all-purpose flour, unsifted**
1 **cup (½ lb.) butter, at room temperature**
1 **egg yolk, beaten with 1 tablespoon milk**

In a large bowl, dissolve yeast in water. Stir in milk, sugar, and salt. Beat in about 2½ cups of the flour to make a soft dough. Turn dough onto a floured board; knead until smooth and satiny (5 to 20 minutes), adding flour as needed to prevent sticking.

Turn dough over in a greased bowl; cover and let rise in a warm place until doubled (about 2 hours). Punch dough down; knead briefly on a lightly floured board to release air.

Roll on floured board to form a large rectangle about ¼ inch thick. Cut butter into slices (it should be just soft enough to spread on a firm bread, but not meltingly soft) and arrange slices in center ⅓ section of dough rectangle. Fold each extending side over butter, pressing the open edges together to seal. Roll out again on floured board until rectangle is about ⅜ inch thick. If at any time dough oozes butter and becomes sticky while you're rolling it, refrigerate until butter is firmer. While rolling, turn dough over occasionally, flouring board lightly to prevent sticking. Fold in thirds again to make a squarish rectangle. Roll dough and fold again the same way.

Wrap dough in clear plastic wrap and refrigerate for 15 to 30 minutes. Roll and fold again 2 more times exactly as directed before. Refrigerate wrapped dough again, for 15 to 30 minutes.

Roll dough into a rectangle that is ⅛ inch thick. Cut in triangles approximately 6 inches at base and 8 inches on 2 remaining sides. Roll up each triangle of dough from 6-inch edge, pinching tip securely to middle section of roll. Shape each roll into a crescent (tighter than a half-circle) and, with sealed point down, place on an ungreased baking sheet about 1½ inches apart all around. Cover and let rise in a warm place until almost doubled (about 2 hours).

Brush each gently with egg yolk-milk mixture. Bake in a 375° oven for 25 minutes or until golden brown. Serve hot, or let cool on racks. Freeze to store. Makes about 18 croissants.

To duplicate the French style, bake croissants 5 to 7 minutes longer—croissants served in Paris are usually a deep brown.

To partially bake croissants for final baking later, bake in a 375° oven for 18 minutes. Let cool on racks, package airtight, and keep in refrigerator. Just before serving, complete the baking in a 375° oven for 12 to 15 minutes or until rolls are golden brown.

Quick Butter Croissants

We have discovered a remarkably simple method of making croissants that closely resemble the traditional ones the French serve for breakfast (see preceding recipe). You cut firm butter into flour (as you would when making baking powder biscuits), then blend this mixture with a yeast batter. The resulting dough is marbled with pockets of butter that form flaky layers when the croissants are baked. *(Photograph on page 35.)*

You can store the dough in the refrigerator up to 4 days, until you're ready to shape and bake the rolls.

    1 package active dry yeast
    1 cup warm water (about 110°)
    ¾ cup evaporated milk
    1½ teaspoons salt
    ⅓ cup sugar
    1 egg
    5¼ to 5½ cups all-purpose flour, unsifted
    ¼ cup butter or margarine, melted and
         cooled
    1 cup (½ lb.) firm butter or margarine, at
         refrigerator temperature
    1 egg beaten with 1 tablespoon water

In a large bowl, dissolve yeast in water. Add milk, salt, sugar, egg, and 1 cup of the flour. Beat to make a smooth batter, then blend in melted butter; set aside.

In a large bowl, using a pastry blender or 2 knives, cut the 1 cup firm butter into 4 cups of the remaining flour until butter particles are the size of peas. Pour yeast batter over top and carefully turn mixture over with a spatula to blend just until all flour is moistened. Cover with clear plastic wrap and refrigerate for at least 4 hours or up to 4 days.

Turn dough out onto a floured board, press into a compact ball, and knead briefly on a lightly floured board to release air. Divide dough into 4 equal parts. Shape 1 part at a time, leaving remaining dough, wrapped in plastic wrap, in refrigerator.

On a floured board, roll 1 part of dough at a time into a circle, 17 inches in diameter. Using a sharp knife, cut circle into 8 equal wedges.

For each croissant, loosely roll wedges toward point. Shape each roll into a crescent and place on an ungreased baking sheet with point down, 1½ inches apart all around. Cover lightly and let rise at room temperature in a draft-free place. (Do not speed rising of rolls by placing them in a warm spot.)

When almost doubled (about 2 hours), brush with egg-water mixture. Bake in a 325° oven for about 35 minutes or until lightly browned. Serve warm, or let cool on racks. Makes 32 croissants.

To reheat, arrange rolls (thawed, if frozen) in single layer on baking sheet; place, uncovered, in a 350° oven for about 10 minutes.

Finnish Hiivaleipa

This round, grainy bread from Finland can be made with either rye or whole wheat flour. To vary it, you might try a combination of the two. The Finns usually cut it in wedges, split each wedge, and serve it with butter. Pronounce it *"hee-vah-lay-pah."*

    1½ cups hot water
    2 tablespoons butter or margarine
    1 tablespoon sugar
    2 teaspoons salt
    1 package active dry yeast
    ½ cup warm water (about 110°)
    3 cups whole wheat or rye flour, unsifted
    2½ to 3 cups all-purpose flour, unsifted

Measure hot water into a large bowl. Stir in butter, sugar, and salt. Set aside to cool until warm (about 110°).

Meanwhile, dissolve yeast in the ½ cup warm water, then blend into first mixture. Beat in whole wheat or rye flour, then gradually stir in about 2 cups of the all-purpose flour to make a stiff dough. Turn dough out onto a floured board; knead until smooth and elastic (10 to 20 minutes), adding flour as needed to prevent sticking. Turn dough over in a greased bowl; cover and let rise in a warm place until doubled (about 1 hour).

(Continued on page 39)

Baguettes (page 34), Bolillos (page 42), and Bagels (page 41) make crusty picnic breads to break and eat with meat and cheese.

. . . Finnish Hiivaleipa (cont'd.)

Punch dough down and knead briefly on a lightly floured board to release air. Divide in half and shape each half into a round loaf. Place loaves on lightly greased baking sheets; press down each loaf until it is about 1 inch thick. Cover and let rise until almost doubled (about 45 minutes).

Bake in a 400° oven for 25 to 30 minutes or until crust is light brown and loaves sound hollow when tapped. Cool on racks. Makes 2 loaves.

Finnish Farmer Bread

This curiously shaped loaf snaps apart into long "fingers" of chewy rye-wheat. The original recipe called for rye meal—a coarse pumpernickel-type rye that's available in some health food stores—and if you are especially fond of heavy, firm breads, you may prefer the bread made with rye meal. Allow a little more time for this heavier grain to rise, as the recipe indicates.

    1 package active dry yeast
 1½ teaspoons sugar
 1¼ cups warm water (about 110°)
 1½ teaspoons salt
    2 teaspoons salad oil
    2 tablespoons caraway seed (optional)
 1½ cups rye flour or rye meal, unsifted
 1¾ to 2 cups all-purpose flour, unsifted
       About 2 tablespoons butter or margarine,
          melted

In a large bowl, combine yeast, sugar, and water; let stand until bubbly (about 15 minutes). Stir in salt, oil, and caraway seed. Then add ½ cup *each* of the rye flour or meal and all-purpose flour; beat until smooth.

Beat in remaining 1 cup rye flour or meal; then gradually mix in about 1 cup of the remaining all-purpose flour to make a stiff dough. Turn dough out onto a floured board; knead until smooth and elastic (5 to 20 minutes), adding flour as needed to prevent sticking.

Turn dough over in a greased bowl; cover and let rise in a warm place until doubled (about 45 minutes; if rye meal is used, allow about 1 hour, 15 minutes).

Punch dough down, knead briefly on a lightly floured board to release air, and divide in half. Shape each into a smooth ball on a lightly floured board. Then pat into a circle about 8 or 9 inches in diameter. Place on a greased rimless baking sheet or on bottom of an inverted rimmed baking pan. Cover loosely and let rise until almost doubled (about 40 minutes; if rye meal is used, allow about 1 hour, 15 minutes).

Using handle of a long wooden spoon, press straight down through loaves to pan in rows about 1 inch apart. Brush tops of loaves lightly with part of the melted butter. Bake in a 375° oven for about 35 minutes or until bread is well browned and sounds hollow when tapped. To bake both loaves in same oven, arrange pans in different positions on 2 oven racks; for good heat circulation, keep pan edges at least an inch from sides of oven. About halfway through baking, switch positions of pans.

Remove bread from oven; brush tops of loaves with remaining melted butter. Cool slightly on racks. Makes 2 loaves.

Make creases about 1 inch apart by pressing dough with long handle of wooden spoon.

Limpa

This hearty rye bread—an old tradition in Sweden—is flavored with fennel and grated orange peel. Wonderful with just butter and a mild cheese, a sliced loaf of limpa could also be turned into a trayful of assorted Scandinavian open-faced sandwiches.

    1 cup boiling water
    ½ cup cracked wheat
    2 teaspoons crushed fennel seed
    1 tablespoon grated orange peel
    2 teaspoons salt
    ⅓ cup molasses
    3 tablespoons butter or margarine
    1 package active dry yeast
    ¼ cup warm water (about 110°)
    1 cup milk, at room temperature
    2 cups rye flour, unsifted
    4 to 4½ cups all-purpose flour, unsifted
       Butter or margarine, melted

In a large bowl, pour boiling water over cracked wheat, fennel seed, orange peel, salt, molasses, and butter; let cool to lukewarm. Meanwhile, dissolve yeast in the ¼ cup water; then stir into lukewarm mixture. Beat in milk and rye flour; then gradually stir in about 3½ cups of the all-purpose flour to make a moderately stiff dough.

Turn dough out onto a floured board and knead until smooth and elastic (10 to 20 minutes), adding flour as needed to prevent sticking. Turn dough over in a greased bowl; cover and let rise in a warm place until doubled (about 2 hours). Punch dough down; knead briefly on a lightly floured board to release air. Divide in half; shape each half into a round loaf about 9 inches in diameter. Place each on a greased baking sheet. Cover and let rise in a warm place until almost doubled (about 1 hour).

Bake in a 350° oven for about 35 minutes (switch pan positions halfway through baking) or until loaves sound hollow when tapped. Brush tops with melted butter. Cool on racks. Makes 2 loaves.

Challah

This festive, seed-studded braid with its glossy brown crust and delicate flavor is called *challah* (pronounced and sometimes spelled "hallah"). Now a popular delicatessen item, challah has long-standing religious significance for the Jewish people, who enjoy it on the Sabbath and often adorn it with a sugar glaze and candied fruit or candies for special holidays. *(Photograph on page 43.)*

  1 **package active dry yeast**
1¼ **cups warm water (about 110°)**
  1 **teaspoon salt**
 ¼ **cup *each* sugar and salad oil**
  2 **eggs, slightly beaten**
  2 **or 3 drops yellow food coloring, or pinch**
     of saffron
  5 **to 5½ cups all-purpose flour, unsifted**
  1 **egg yolk beaten with 1 tablespoon water**
     About 1 tablespoon sesame seed or poppy
     seed

In a large bowl, dissolve yeast in water. Stir in salt, sugar, oil, eggs, and food coloring. Gradually beat in about 4½ cups of the flour to make a stiff dough.

Turn dough out onto a floured board and knead until smooth and satiny (5 to 20 minutes), adding flour as needed to prevent sticking. Turn dough over in a greased bowl; cover and let rise in a warm place until doubled (about 1½ hours). Punch dough down; knead briefly on a lightly floured board to release air. Set aside and cover about ¾ cup dough.

Divide remaining dough into 4 equal portions; roll each between hands to form a strand about 20 inches long. Place the 4 strips lengthwise on a greased baking sheet, pinch tops together, and braid as follows: pick up strand on right, bring it over next one, under the third, and over the fourth. Repeat, always starting with strand on right, until braid is complete. Pinch ends together.

Roll reserved dough into a strip about 15 inches long; cut into 3 strips and make a small 3-strand braid. Lay on top center of large braid. Cover and let rise in a warm place until almost doubled (about 1 hour).

Using a soft brush or your fingers, spread egg yolk mixture evenly over braids; sprinkle with seed. Bake in a 350° oven for 30 to 35 minutes or until loaf is golden brown and sounds hollow when tapped. Serve warm, or let cool on rack. Makes 1 loaf.

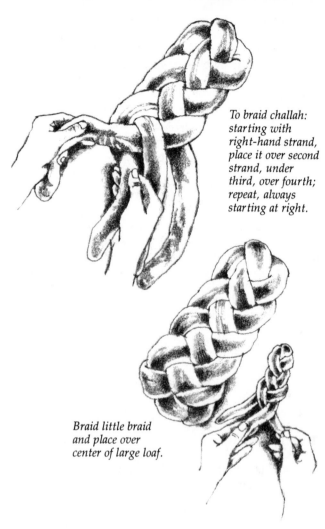

To braid challah: starting with right-hand strand, place it over second strand, under third, over fourth; repeat, always starting at right.

Braid little braid and place over center of large loaf.

Soft Pretzels

German soft pretzels are crusty but have a more breadlike interior than commercial crisp pretzels. Though they are best the day you bake them, you can freeze extras, then reheat to serve. Try them warm with butter or your favorite spicy mustard.

   1 **package active dry yeast**
   1 **cup warm water (about 110°)**
2½ **to 2¾ cups all-purpose flour, unsifted**
   2 **tablespoons salad oil**
   1 **tablespoon sugar**
   6 **cups water with 6 tablespoons soda**
      Coarse salt

In a bowl, dissolve yeast in water. Add 1½ cups of the flour, the oil, and sugar. Beat for about 3 minutes to make a smooth batter. Gradually stir in enough of the remaining flour (about 1 cup) to form a soft dough. Turn out onto a floured board and knead until smooth and satiny (about 5 minutes), adding flour as needed to prevent sticking. Turn dough over in a greased bowl; cover and let rise in a warm place until doubled (about 1 hour).

Punch dough down, turn out onto floured board, and divide into 12 pieces. Shape each into a smooth ball by gently kneading. Then roll each into a smooth rope about 18 inches long and twist into a pretzel shape. Place pretzels, slightly apart, on a greased baking sheet, tucking ends underneath. Let rise, uncovered, until puffy (about 25 minutes).

In a 3-quart stainless steel or enameled pan (do not use aluminum), bring water-soda mixture to boiling; adjust heat to keep water boiling gently. With a slotted spatula, lower 1 pretzel at a time into pan. Let simmer for 10 seconds on each side, then lift from water, drain briefly, and place on a greased baking sheet. Let dry briefly, then sprinkle with coarse salt. Let stand, uncovered, until all have been simmered.

Bake in a 425° oven for about 12 to 15 minutes or until golden brown. Transfer to racks; serve warm with butter or mustard. Or cool completely, wrap airtight, and freeze. Reheat, uncovered, in a 350° oven for about 10 minutes or until warm. Makes 1 dozen pretzels.

Basic Bagels

Like many traditional breads, the bagel has a long, romantic history. According to legend, a Viennese baker invented it in 1683 as a tribute to Polish Prince John Soviesky, who had rescued the city from invading Turks. Originally called a "beugal," it was shaped like the prince's stirrup. *(Photograph on page 38.)*

- 2 **packages active dry yeast**
- 2 **cups warm water (about 110°)**
- 3 **tablespoons sugar**
- 3 **teaspoons salt**
- 5½ **to 6 cups all-purpose flour, unsifted**
- 3 **quarts water with 1 tablespoon sugar**
- **Cornmeal**
- 1 **egg yolk beaten with 1 tablespoon water**

In a large bowl, dissolve yeast in water. Stir in sugar and salt; gradually mix in 4 cups of the flour. Beat well to make a smooth batter. Mix in about 1¼ cups more flour to make a stiff dough.

Turn dough out onto a floured board and knead until smooth and elastic (10 to 20 minutes), adding flour as needed to prevent sticking—dough should be firmer than for most other yeast breads. Turn dough over in a greased bowl; cover and let rise in a warm place until doubled (about 40 minutes).

Punch dough down; knead briefly on a lightly floured board to release air, then divide into 18 equal

pieces. To shape, knead each piece, forming it into a smooth ball. Holding ball with both hands, poke your thumbs through center. With one thumb in the hole, work around perimeter, shaping bagel like a doughnut, 2½ to 3 inches across. Place shaped bagels on a lightly floured board, cover lightly, and let stand in a warm place for 20 minutes.

Bring water-sugar mixture to boiling in a 4 or 5-quart pan; adjust heat to keep it boiling gently. Lightly grease a baking sheet and sprinkle with cornmeal. Gently lift one bagel at a time and drop into water; boil about 5 or 6 at a time, turning often, for 5 minutes. Lift out with a slotted spatula, drain briefly on a towel, and place on baking sheet.

Brush bagels with egg yolk mixture. Bake in a 400° oven for about 25 to 30 minutes or until well browned and crusty. Cool on a rack. Makes 18 bagels.

Whole Wheat Bagels

Follow recipe for Basic Bagels (left), omitting the 3 tablespoons sugar; use 3 tablespoons **honey** instead. In place of the flour use 2 cups **whole wheat** or **graham flour,** ½ cup **wheat germ,** and about 2¾ cups **all-purpose flour** (all unsifted). Mix in all the whole wheat flour and wheat germ and 1¼ cups of the all-purpose flour before beating dough. Then mix in about 1½ cups more all-purpose flour; knead and finish as directed.

Pumpernickel Bagels

Follow recipe for Basic Bagels (left), omitting the 3 tablespoons sugar; use 3 tablespoons dark **molasses** instead. In place of the flour use 2 cups **rye flour,** 2 cups **whole wheat** or **graham flour,** and about 1¾ cups **all-purpose flour** (all unsifted). Add all the rye and 1 cup *each* of the whole wheat and all-purpose flour before beating dough. Then add remaining 1 cup whole wheat and about ¾ cup more all-purpose flour; knead and finish as directed.

More Bagel Variety

Try adding ½ cup instant toasted **onion** to Whole Wheat or Basic Bagels (left)—add it to yeast mixture along with sugar and salt. Or sprinkle ½ teaspoon **poppy seed** or **sesame seed** or ¼ teaspoon **coarse salt** on each glazed bagel before baking. Or add 1 tablespoon **caraway seed** to Pumpernickel Bagels (above), then sprinkle each glazed bagel with ½ teaspoon more **caraway seed** before baking.

Basque Sheepherder's Bread

This vast, dome-shaped loaf is a Basque sheepherder's staff of life. Before serving, a herder's custom is to slash the sign of the cross in the top of the bread, then serve the first piece to his invaluable dog.

Many Basques still bake it in a cast-iron Dutch oven in a pit under a campfire. Our method of baking it in a conventional oven is more reliable (if less exciting)—but to achieve the characteristic shape, you'll still need a 10-inch cast-iron or cast-aluminum covered Dutch oven (5-qt. size). *(Photograph on page 46.)*

- 3 **cups very hot tap water**
- ½ **cup (¼ lb.) butter or margarine**
- ⅓ **cup sugar**
- 2½ **teaspoons salt**
- 2 **packages active dry yeast**
- 9 **to 9½ cups all-purpose flour, unsifted**
  Salad oil

In a large bowl, combine hot water, butter, sugar, and salt. Stir until butter melts; let cool to about 110°. Stir in yeast, cover, and set in a warm place until bubbly (about 15 minutes).

Beat in about 5 cups of the flour to make a thick batter. Stir in enough of the remaining flour (about 3½ cups) to make a stiff dough. Turn dough out onto a floured board; knead until smooth and satiny (10 to 20 minutes), adding flour as needed to prevent sticking. Turn dough over in a greased bowl, cover, and let rise in a warm place until doubled (about 1½ hours).

Punch dough down and knead on a floured board to form a smooth ball. With a circle of foil, cover the inside bottom of Dutch oven. Grease foil, inside of Dutch oven, and underside of lid with salad oil.

Place dough in pot and cover with lid. Let rise in a warm place until dough pushes up lid by about ½ inch (about 1 hour—watch closely).

Bake, covered with lid, in a 375° oven for 12 minutes. Remove lid and bake for another 30 to 35 minutes or until loaf is golden brown and sounds hollow when tapped. Remove from oven and turn loaf out (you'll need a helper) onto a rack to cool. Peel off foil. Makes 1 very large loaf.

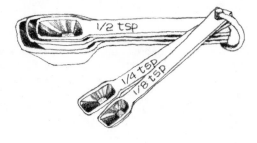

A glorious golden loaf is worth rounds of applause. This one is a braided Challah (page 40).

Bolillos

Travelers in Mexico soon discover that tortillas are not the only bread served there. One plain yeast roll, called *bolillo* (pronounced bow-*le*-yo) is just as popular. It has a crisp, chewy crust similar to our hard French roll.

In place of sliced bread or dinner rolls, bolillos can be served several ways; try them split in half for cold sandwiches, or as a bread accompaniment with salads or bowls of soup or stew. *(Photograph on page 38.)*

- 2 **cups water**
- 1½ **tablespoons sugar**
- 1 **tablespoon salt**
- 2 **tablespoons butter or margarine**
- 1 **package active dry yeast**
- 5½ **to 6 cups all-purpose flour, unsifted**
- 1 **teaspoon cornstarch dissolved in ½ cup water**

In a pan, combine water, sugar, salt, and butter. Warm over low heat, stirring, to about 110°. Pour into a large bowl; stir in yeast until dissolved. Gradually beat in about 5 cups of the flour to make a stiff dough.

Turn dough out onto a floured board and knead until smooth and satiny (5 to 20 minutes), adding flour as needed to prevent sticking. Turn dough over in a greased bowl; cover and let rise in a warm place until doubled (about 1½ hours).

Punch dough down; knead briefly on a lightly floured board to release air. Divide into 16 equal pieces. Form each piece into a smooth ball by gently kneading; then shape each ball into an oblong by rolling it and gently pulling from center to ends until it is about 4 inches long (center should be thicker than ends). Place rolls 3 inches apart on greased baking sheets; you need 3 pans, each about 12 by 15 inches.

In a standard-size oven with 2 racks, you can bake 2 sheets of rolls at a time. If you have only 1 oven, cover third pan of shaped bolillos with clear plastic wrap and refrigerate for up to 30 minutes. Cover rolls and let rise until almost doubled (about 35 minutes—or 45 minutes if refrigerated).

In a pan, heat cornstarch and water to boiling; cool slightly. Brush each roll with cornstarch mixture; then with a razor blade or a sharp floured knife, cut a slash about ¾ inch deep and about 2 inches long in top of each roll.

Adjust oven racks so they are equally spaced in oven from top to bottom, then stagger baking sheets to get best heat distribution. Bake in a 375° oven for 35 to 40 minutes or until rolls are golden brown and sound hollow when tapped (switch pans halfway through baking). Cool on racks. Makes 16 rolls.

Armenian Thin Bread

Thin and crackly, these big, bubbly rounds snap apart into serving-size pieces. Sesame seed, whole wheat flour, and wheat germ give them a delicious, nutty flavor.

Each of the rounds must be hand-rolled until very thin, but the dough is easy to handle and two breads can bake at once. *(Photograph on page 46.)*

    2 packages active dry yeast
    2 cups warm water (about 110°)
    2 tablespoons sugar
    1 tablespoon salt
    ½ cup (¼ lb.) butter or margarine, melted
        and cooled
 2½ cups whole wheat flour, unsifted
    ½ cup wheat germ
    3 to 3½ cups all-purpose flour, unsifted
    1 egg beaten with ¼ cup cold water
        About ¾ cup sesame seed

In a large bowl, dissolve yeast in water. Stir in sugar, salt, and butter. Add whole wheat flour, wheat germ, and 1 cup of the all-purpose flour; beat until well blended and stretchy. Then stir in about 1½ cups of the remaining all-purpose flour to make a stiff dough.

Turn dough out onto a floured board and knead until smooth and satiny (5 to 20 minutes), adding flour as needed to prevent sticking. Turn dough over in a greased bowl; cover and let rise in a warm place until doubled (1 to 1½ hours).

Punch dough down, knead briefly on a lightly floured board to release air, then divide into 12 equal pieces. Shape each piece into a smooth ball and place about 1 inch apart on a lightly floured board or baking sheet. Cover and let rest at room temperature for at least 45 minutes.

Arrange oven racks so that one is at lowest level and the other at highest level of your oven.

Roll out 1 ball of dough at a time on a lightly floured board to a 10 by 12-inch oval—it will be almost paper thin. Carefully transfer to an ungreased baking sheet. Brush lightly with egg-water mixture and sprinkle with about 1 tablespoon sesame seed. Prick surface 3 or 4 times with a fork.

Bake on lowest rack of a 400° oven for about 4 minutes, then move to top rack and bake for another 4 minutes or until golden brown and puffy. As you move first bread to top rack, place another bread on bottom rack. Continue in this way until all are baked. Cool briefly on racks, then stack. Makes 12 breads.

White Flour Thin Bread

Follow recipe for Armenian Thin Bread (left), but instead of mixture of flours, use about 6 cups **all-purpose flour** (unsifted), adding 4 cups in first addition and remaining flour as directed.

Peda Bread I

The Armenian bread called *peda* looks like an oversized doughnut baked by someone too frugal to discard the hole in the center. Our version of this flat sesame-seeded loaf is simpler to make than most yeast breads. After mixing and shaping the dough, you refrigerate it for 2 to 24 hours and then bake just before serving. *(Photograph on page 46.)*

    2 packages active dry yeast
    ½ cup warm water (about 110°)
 1¾ cups warm milk (about 110°)
    2 tablespoons sugar
    1 teaspoon salt
    3 tablespoons olive oil
    6 to 6½ cups all-purpose flour, unsifted
        Olive oil
    1 egg yolk beaten with 1 tablespoon water
    4 tablespoons sesame seed

In a large bowl, dissolve yeast in water. Stir in milk, sugar, salt, and olive oil. Gradually beat in about 5½ cups of the flour to make a stiff dough. Turn dough out onto a floured board and knead until smooth and elastic (5 to 20 minutes), adding flour as needed to prevent sticking.

Cover dough and let rest at room temperature for 20 minutes. Knead on a lightly floured board to release air, then pinch off 2 small portions of dough, each about ½-cup size, and divide large piece of dough in half. Shape each portion into a smooth ball.

To make each loaf, flatten a large piece of dough on a greased baking sheet into a flat round cake; poke a

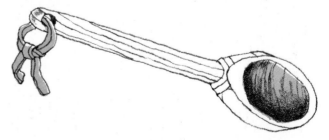

hole in the center and, with your fingers pulling in opposition, make a 4-inch-diameter hole; flatten dough rim to make it 10 inches in diameter. Place 1 of the small balls of dough in center and flatten gently to fill hole. Brush lightly with olive oil; repeat to make second loaf. Cover dough with clear plastic wrap and refrigerate for 2 to 24 hours.

When ready to bake, remove loaf or loaves from refrigerator, uncover, and let stand at room temperature for 10 minutes. Brush each loaf with egg yolk-water mixture and sprinkle with 2 tablespoons sesame seed.

Bake in a 350° oven for 35 minutes or until crust is a deep golden color and loaves sound hollow when tapped. Cool on racks. Makes 2 large loaves.

To bake freshly made dough, shape, oil, and let stand at room temperature, lightly covered, for 20 minutes; then brush with egg yolk-water mixture, top with sesame seed, and bake as directed.

Peda Bread II

There are many versions of *peda.* This one closely resembles the flat, chewy loaves made in Armenian bakeries in Los Angeles. Delicious with meat, this peda can be adapted several ways—even to make hamburger buns (see variations following recipe). *(Photograph on page 46.)*

- 2 **packages active dry yeast**
- 2 **cups warm water (about 110°)**
- 2 **tablespoons sugar**
- 1 **tablespoon salt**
- 3 **tablespoons butter or margarine (melted) or salad oil**
- 5½ **to 6 cups all-purpose flour, unsifted**
  Flour glaze (recipe follows)
  About 2 teaspoons toasted sesame seed or poppy seed (optional)

In a large bowl, dissolve yeast in water. Stir in sugar, salt, and butter. Gradually beat in about 5 cups of the flour to make a stiff dough.

Turn dough out onto a floured board and knead until smooth and satiny (5 to 20 minutes), adding flour as needed to prevent sticking. Turn dough over in a greased bowl; cover and let rise in a warm place until doubled (about 1 hour).

Lightly grease 2 large baking sheets and dust with flour. Punch dough down, divide into 2 equal parts, and shape each into a smooth ball. Set each ball on a baking sheet, cover lightly, and let rest at room temperature for 30 minutes. Then press, pull, and pound with your fist to shape each loaf into an oval about 11 by 14 inches (if too elastic to hold shape, let rest a few minutes longer). Cover and let rise in a warm place until doubled (45 to 60 minutes).

Using a soft brush dipped in cool water, brush top and sides of each loaf. Then dip finger tips in water and, with the 4 finger tips of each hand lined up,

mark bread like this: press down to metal pan, marking first a 1½-inch-wide border around edge, then lines crosswise and lengthwise, about 2 inches apart (see below). Let rise, uncovered, until almost doubled (about 45 minutes). Meanwhile, prepare flour glaze.

Bake 1 loaf at a time in center of a 450° oven for about 15 minutes or until golden brown. As each loaf comes from oven, apply glaze lightly over sides and top with a soft brush. If you wish to add seeds, repaint each loaf lightly with glaze and immediately sprinkle with seeds. Cool on racks. Makes 2 large loaves.

Flour glaze. In a small pan, blend 2 teaspoons **flour** with ½ cup cold **water** until smooth. Place over medium heat and cook, stirring, until mixture boils and thickens. Remove from heat and let stand, covered, until ready to use.

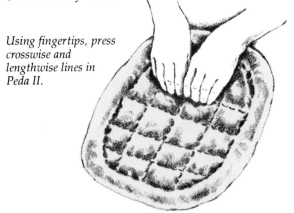

Using fingertips, press crosswise and lengthwise lines in Peda II.

Whole Wheat Peda

Follow the recipe for Peda Bread II (left), using 2½ cups **whole wheat flour** (unsifted), ½ cup **wheat germ**, and only about 2½ cups **all-purpose flour** (unsifted). Add all the whole wheat flour and wheat germ and 1 cup all-purpose flour in first mixing stage. Mix in remaining all-purpose flour and finish as directed.

Mini-Loaves of Peda

Prepare regular or whole wheat Peda Bread II as directed in preceding recipes, except after dough rises first time, divide it into 12 equal pieces. Shape each into a smooth ball and place on greased and floured baking sheets (6 rolls on each sheet). Let rest for 30 minutes, then flatten each ball to about 4½ inches in diameter. Omit brushing with water and marking. After loaves have risen until almost doubled, bake in a 425° oven for about 15 minutes or until golden brown. Remove from oven and immediately brush on flour glaze; if desired, repaint and sprinkle with seeds. Makes 12 mini-loaves.

Arab Pocket Bread

These individual-size rounds of Arab bread puff and form pockets as they bake. In the Middle East, they are commonly served as tidy and tasty containers for savory meat fillings and yogurt. To use them this way, just tear or cut them open and fill the pockets.

Depending on the size of your oven and pans, you can bake three to five loaves at a time. You'll need two or three baking sheets, large cloths, and light plastic to cover breads while they rest and rise—a torn piece of sheet or tea towels and a plastic garment bag work well. A large terry cloth bath towel is handy to cool the hot breads on. *(Photograph on facing page.)*

1 package active dry yeast
1 tablespoon sugar
3 cups warm water (about 110°)
1 tablespoon *each* salt and salad oil
9 cups all-purpose flour, unsifted

In a small bowl, combine yeast, sugar, and water; let stand until bubbly (about 5 minutes); stir in salt and salad oil. Place all the flour in a large bowl and make a well in center. Pour in about half the yeast mixture at a time. Mix and knead with your hand until flour and liquid hold together.

Turn dough out onto a well-floured board and shape into a log; divide into 20 equal pieces. Place pieces of dough on floured board and keep covered. To shape each loaf, place a piece of dough in a floured palm. With your other hand, pull dough out away from sides, then fold it back toward center and press in middle; work around edge until smooth and elastic. Place smooth side up on cloth-lined trays. Cover with a dry cloth, then top with a damp cloth. Let rise at room temperature until puffy (1 to 1½ hours).

One at a time, place a ball on a floured board. With a rolling pin, flatten, then roll out from center with 4 strokes each way to make a 6-inch round. Shake off excess flour and place rounds at least ½ inch apart on a dry cloth. Cover with another dry cloth, then top with a damp cloth. Cover all with plastic. Let rest at room temperature until slightly puffy (about 1 hour).

Carefully lift and transfer 3 to 5 loaves to an ungreased 12 by 15-inch baking sheet, placing them about ½ inch apart. Adjust oven rack so it is 2 inches from oven bottom.

Bake loaves in a 475° oven until pockets form and bottoms brown lightly (about 5 minutes). Immediately switch oven to broil and move baking sheet to 4 inches below heat. Broil until tops are lightly browned (about 1 minute). Slide loaves off baking sheet onto a towel and let cool thoroughly. After they're cooled, you can gently flatten each, package airtight, and refrigerate or freeze. Thaw frozen loaves and reheat, uncovered, in a 300° oven for about 5 to 10 minutes. Makes 20.

For whole wheat Arab Pocket Bread, prepare Arab Pocket Bread as directed, with this change: reduce all-purpose flour to 5 cups and add 3½ cups **whole wheat flour** and ½ cup **wheat germ**.

Zuñi Bread

The Pueblo peoples of the Southwest share an ancient way of living. Each adds special touches to a style of village life that extends backward to the Basketmakers and Cliff Dwellers.

You'll find in many pueblos a yeast bread like the one here, but this recipe from the Zuñi people is as unique as their burnished black pottery. The village women bake the bread in domed outdoor earth ovens—but your kitchen range will also produce a beautiful, crusty loaf. *(Photograph on facing page.)*

1 package active dry yeast
2 cups warm water (about 110°)
¼ cup *each* salad oil and molasses
2 teaspoons salt
1 cup *each* polenta (coarse-ground Italian-style cornmeal) and yellow cornmeal; or 2 cups yellow cornmeal
6½ to 7 cups all-purpose flour, unsifted

In a large bowl, dissolve yeast in water. Add oil, molasses, salt, polenta, and cornmeal; mix well. Gradually beat in about 6 cups of the flour to make a stiff dough. Turn dough out onto a floured board and knead until smooth and elastic (5 to 20 minutes), adding flour as needed to prevent sticking.

Turn dough over in a greased bowl; cover and let rise in a warm place until doubled (about 1½ hours). Punch dough down; knead briefly on a lightly floured board to release air, and divide in half. Shape each half into a smooth ball.

To shape each loaf, flatten ball into a 9-inch round. Fold the round slightly off-center so top edge is set back about 1 inch from bottom edge. With a razor blade or sharp floured knife, make 4 equally spaced cuts about ⅔ of the way across loaves on curved side.

Place shaped loaves well apart on a greased baking sheet; cover lightly and let rise until almost doubled (about 45 minutes). Bake in a 375° oven for about 30 to 35 minutes or until loaves are a rich golden brown. Let cool on racks. Makes 2 large loaves.

Adventures with Sourdough

Classic Sourdough French Bread (page 52).

For generations, sourdough has mystified cooks and aroused their curiosity. Many stories have been told about early pioneers and the measures they often took to guard the ingredients of their sourdough starter—the mysterious self-replenishing substance that gave them sure-fire hotcakes morning after morning. They shared the starter only with worthy friends.

Historians have attempted to trace the origins of sourdough. Some propose that hunters or woodsmen in the midst of preparing breakfast suddenly left camp, leaving their hotcake batter sitting by the fire. Days later they may have found it curiously full of bubbles, exuding a good sour aroma. It probably made the best hotcakes they'd ever tasted. Others suggest that some Egyptian baker discovered this strange fermented substance when he accidentally left a bit of dough out in the sun.

However the phenomenon of sourdough was discovered, it wasn't until recent time that anyone could explain it scientifically. The organisms responsible for sourdough's characteristic flavor have been isolated—the cause is not yeast, but harmless bacteria that are naturally present in raw milk. Unfortunately, they do not always survive pasteurization. The forms of the bacteria essential for sourdough fermentation are also present in products like aged Cheddar cheese, cultured buttermilk, and yogurt.

We tried making starters with all of these products, and decided that yogurt was the easiest to work with. It also gave us the best, most active starters, which, in turn, gave that wonderful zesty flavor and aroma to baked goods.

Sourdough Starter

Start with a 1½-quart glass, pottery, rigid plastic, or stainless steel container. Rinse with hot water for several minutes, then wipe dry.

Heat 1 cup skim or low-fat milk to 90° to 100° on a thermometer (skim gives the most tang). Remove from heat and stir in 3 tablespoons unflavored, low-fat yogurt (any brand). Pour milk into the warm container, cover tightly, and let stand in a warm place. Temperatures of 80° to 100° are ideal (above 110° bacteria may be killed—it could smell sour, but won't get bubbly; below 70°, it doesn't grow well).

Look for a warm place to put the starter. Good spots are on top of water heaters, built-in refrigerators, or other partially enclosed areas where heat collects. If you have a gas range, place the starter on a burner near (but not over) the pilot light.

With an electric oven, you can adjust a rack so top of container will be 2 to 2½ inches under the oven light. Turn oven to lowest setting or just until air inside feels slightly warmer than room temperature; turn oven off. Place container directly in front of (but not touching) the light. Close door and turn light on (or prop door open just enough to keep light on). If room is cold, occasionally remove container and repeat oven warming.

After about 18 to 24 hours, starter should be about the consistency of yogurt (a curd forms and mixture does not flow readily when container is slightly tilted). During this time if some clear liquid rises to top of milk, simply stir it back in. However, if liquid has turned light pink, it indicates that milk is beginning to break down; discard and start again.

After a curd has formed, gradually stir 1 cup all-purpose flour (unsifted) into the starter until smoothly blended. Cover tightly and let stand in a warm place (80° to 100° is ideal) until mixture is full of bubbles and has a good sour smell; this takes 2 to 5 days.

During this time, if clear liquid forms, stir it back into starter. But if liquid turns pink, spoon out and discard all but ¼ cup of starter, then blend in a mixture of 1 cup *each* warm milk (90° to 100°) and flour. Cover tightly and let stand again in a warm place until bubbly and sour-smelling—then it's ready to use. Or cover it and store in refrigerator. This makes about 1½ cups starter.

Should a light growth of mold form on your starter at any time, simply scrape it off and discard. The mold is harmless and is similar to the type that often forms on cheese.

While your starter is "young" (up to six months old), you are more likely to have success with it if you use it in recipes that also include yeast. To maintain an ample supply, each time you use part of your starter replenish it with equal amounts of warm milk (90° to 100°) and flour. (For example, if you use ½ cup starter, blend in a mixture of ½ cup warm milk and ½ cup flour.) Cover and let stand in a warm place several hours or overnight until it is again full of bubbles; then store, covered, in the refrigerator until you use it again. For consistent flavor, continue using the same type of milk you originally used. Always let your starter warm to room temperature before using it; this takes about 4 to 6 hours. If you like to bake in the morning, leave it out the night before.

If you bake regularly—about once a week—the starter should keep lively and active; if you don't, it's best to discard about ½ of your starter and replenish it with warm milk and flour about every two months.

The "feel" of this dough after flour is kneaded in is just slightly tacky when lightly touched.

Sourdough Pancakes and Waffles

Whether your first adventure with sourdough takes place in the kitchen or over a campfire, this is a good recipe to start with.

> 1 cup whole wheat flour, unsifted
> 1 cup all-purpose flour, unsifted
> ½ cup sourdough starter, at room temperature
> 2 cups warm buttermilk (about 110°)
> 2 eggs
> ¼ cup *each* milk and salad oil
> 2 tablespoons sugar
> 1 teaspoon soda
> ½ teaspoon salt
> Melted butter or margarine

In a large bowl, combine whole wheat flour, all-purpose flour, starter, and buttermilk; beat until blended. Cover and let stand at room temperature for about 45 minutes (or cover and refrigerate overnight).

Beat together eggs, milk, and oil. Add to flour mixture and stir until blended. Combine sugar, soda, and salt. Stir into batter, then let stand for 5 minutes.

For waffles, preheat an electric waffle iron. Bake according to manufacturer's directions until richly browned. Serve immediately. Or let cool on wire racks, package airtight, and freeze; reheat frozen waffles in your toaster. Makes 12 waffles, 4 inches square.

For pancakes, drop batter by spoonfuls onto a moderately hot greased griddle; bake until nicely browned on both sides. Makes about 2 dozen pancakes, about 4 inches in diameter.

Sourdough Buckwheats

Follow recipe for Sourdough Pancakes and Waffles (above), but in place of whole wheat flour, substitute ¾ cup **buckwheat flour** and increase **all-purpose flour** to 1¼ cups.

Sourdough Blueberry Pancakes

Follow recipe for Sourdough Pancakes and Waffles (above), stirring in ¾ cup frozen, fresh, or well-drained canned **blueberries** just before baking.

Sourdough Oatmeal Pancakes

Follow recipe for Sourdough Pancakes and Waffles (page 49), substituting 1 cup **rolled oats** for 1 cup of either the whole wheat or the all-purpose flour.

> According to legend, the first waffles were invented quite by accident in medieval Scotland. A tired crusader, waiting for his wife to finish baking his supper of oat cakes, sat down to rest—right on top of some cakes she had left to cool on the bench. His coat of mail imprinted them with a pretty woven pattern, so the couple named the cakes "waffres," which is the Scottish word for woven.

Sourdough Crepes

You can serve these tangy sourdough crepes in all the ways you do regular French crepes. For breakfast, spread them with butter or preserves and sprinkle with sugar. Or for a lunch or dinner entrée, wrap them around a variety of savory fillings.

- ¾ cup sourdough starter, at room temperature
- 1 cup warm water (about 110°)
- 1¼ cups all-purpose flour, unsifted
- 2 eggs
- 3 tablespoons salad oil
- ½ teaspoon *each* salt and soda
- 1 tablespoon sugar
  Butter or margarine

In a bowl, stir together starter, water, and flour until smoothly blended. Cover and let stand in a warm place until very bubbly (about 8 hours).

Beat together eggs and oil, then stir into batter. Also combine salt, soda, and sugar; sprinkle over batter and stir well to blend. Cover lightly and let stand at room temperature for about 15 minutes.

Place a 6 or 7-inch crepe pan or other flat-bottomed frying pan on medium heat. When pan is hot, add ¼ teaspoon butter or margarine and swirl to coat surface. At once, pour in 1½ to 2 tablespoons batter, quickly tilting pan so batter flows over entire flat surface (don't worry if there are a few little holes). Cook until surface appears dry and edge is lightly browned. With a spatula, turn and brown other side. Turn crepe out of pan onto a plate. Repeat, stacking crepes, until all batter is used. If you do not use the baked crepes within a few hours, cool, package airtight, and refrigerate for as long as a week. Let crepes warm to room temperature before separating them; they tear if cold. Makes 12 to 16 crepes.

Creamy Sourdough Starter (page 48) puts magic flavor into (clockwise from lower left) Cornmeal Bread (page 53), round Potato Bread (page 55), Rye Bread (page 53), French Bread (page 52), and Whole Wheat Pan Bread and braided Potato Bread (both on page 55).

Tangy Sourdough English Muffins

If you haven't tried making your own English muffins before, you'll be pleased to find they're as easy as most breads. They bake very slowly on a griddle or frying pan instead of in the oven.

- 1 package active dry yeast
- ¼ cup warm water (about 110°)
- 1 cup warm milk (about 110°)
- ½ cup sourdough starter, at room temperature
- 1 tablespoon sugar
- ¾ teaspoon salt
- 3½ to 4 cups all-purpose flour, unsifted
  About ¼ cup yellow cornmeal

In a large bowl, dissolve yeast in water. Stir in milk, starter, sugar, salt, and enough of the flour (about 3½ cups) to make a stiff dough. Turn dough out onto a floured board; knead until smooth (5 to 10 minutes), adding flour as needed to prevent sticking. Turn dough over in a greased bowl; cover and let rise in a warm place until doubled (1 to 1½ hours).

Punch dough down and turn out onto a board lightly covered with cornmeal. Roll out or pat dough until it is about ½ inch thick. With a floured 3-inch cooky cutter (or tuna can with both ends removed), cut dough into rounds. Place muffins (cornmeal side up) about 2 inches apart on ungreased baking sheets lightly sprinkled with cornmeal. Cover lightly and let rise in a warm place until puffy (about 45 minutes).

On a lightly greased electric griddle (preheated to 275°) or in a lightly greased large frying pan over low heat, bake muffins until golden brown (about 10 minutes on each side). Cool on racks. Makes 12 to 14 muffins.

Sourdough Whole Grain English Muffins

Sourdough starter puts zest into these hearty, mixed-grain muffins. But, if you prefer, you can also make them without the sour flavor—just omit the starter and use two packages of active dry yeast dissolved in 1⅔ cups water in place of the first three ingredients in the recipe. Expect the dough to rise a bit faster.

(Continued on page 52)

1 **package active dry yeast**
1⅓ **cups warm water (about 110°)**
1 **cup sourdough starter, at room
    temperature**
2 **tablespoons honey**
2 **teaspoons salt**
½ **cup instant nonfat dry milk**
¼ **cup wheat germ**
½ **cup cracked wheat, rolled oats, or mixed
    grain cereal**
1½ **cups whole wheat or graham flour,
    unsifted**
2¾ **to 3 cups all-purpose flour, unsifted
    About ¼ cup yellow cornmeal**

In a large bowl, dissolve yeast in water. Stir in starter, honey, salt, dry milk, wheat germ, cracked wheat (or other cereal), whole wheat or graham flour, and 1 cup of the all-purpose flour. Beat well for 5 minutes. Gradually mix in 1½ cups of the remaining all-purpose flour to make a stiff dough.

Turn dough out onto floured board; knead until smooth (10 to 20 minutes), adding flour as needed to prevent sticking. Turn dough over in a greased bowl; cover and let rise in a warm place until doubled (about 2 hours).

Punch dough down and turn out on a board lightly sprinkled with cornmeal. With a rolling pin, roll out dough to a thickness of about ½ inch. With a floured 3-inch cooky cutter (or tuna can with both ends removed), cut dough in rounds. Place muffins, cornmeal side up, about 1 inch apart on a baking sheet lightly sprinkled with cornmeal. Cover lightly and let rise in a warm place until puffy (about 1 hour).

On a lightly greased electric griddle (preheated to 275°) or in a lightly greased heavy frying pan over low heat, bake muffins until golden brown (12 to 15 minutes on each side). Cool on racks. Makes 1 dozen muffins.

Classic Sourdough French Bread

Rivaling the best of San Francisco sourdough, this tangy, crusty loaf can turn a simple wine-and-cheese picnic into a sumptuous feast. Or, on a cold day, serve it with a hearty soup or stew. It's so delicious, it doesn't even need butter. *(Photographs on pages 51 and 54.)*

2 **cups warm water (about 110°)**
1 **cup sourdough starter, at room
    temperature**
7½ **to 8 cups all-purpose flour, unsifted**
2 **teaspoons *each* salt and sugar
    Cornmeal
    Boiling water**
1 **teaspoon cornstarch mixed with ½ cup
    water**

In a large bowl, combine water, starter, and 4 cups of the flour; stir until smooth. Cover bowl with clear plastic wrap and let stand in a warm place (about 85°) for 6 to 8 hours or until mixture is full of bubbles and spongy-looking.

Stir in salt, sugar, and enough of the remaining flour (about 3 cups) to form a very stiff dough. Turn dough out onto floured board; knead until smooth (10 to 20 minutes), adding flour as needed to prevent sticking. Turn dough over in a greased bowl; cover and let rise in a warm place until doubled (2 to 2½ hours).

Punch dough down and divide in half. Knead each piece gently on a floured board just until dough has a smooth surface. If you have only 1 oven, wrap half the dough in clear plastic wrap and refrigerate.

For an oblong loaf, shape dough into a smooth log by rolling it back and forth, gently elongating loaf to about 14 inches. Sprinkle a piece of stiff cardboard (about 7 by 18 inches) with 3 tablespoons cornmeal and set loaf on top.

For a round loaf, shape dough into a smooth ball. Place loaf on a 12-inch-square piece of stiff cardboard sprinkled with 3 tablespoons cornmeal.

Cover loaves lightly; let rise in a warm place until puffy and almost doubled (1 to 1½ hours). With oven racks in the 2 lowest positions, place a baking sheet on top rack as oven preheats to 400°. Just before bread is ready to bake, place a rimmed baking sheet on lowest rack and pour in boiling water about ¼ inch deep.

Meanwhile, heat cornstarch and water to boiling, stirring; cool slightly. With a razor blade or sharp floured knife, cut ½-inch-deep slashes in top of loaf—3 slightly slanting slashes in oblong loaf, 4 slashes in a crisscross pattern in round loaf. Then brush top and sides evenly with cornstarch mixture. Carefully slide loaf from cardboard onto baking sheet in oven.

Bake at 400° for 10 minutes; then brush evenly again with cornstarch mixture. Bake for 20 to 25 minutes longer or until loaves are golden brown and sound hollow when tapped. Cool on racks. Makes 2 loaves.

When you put first loaf in oven, remove second piece of dough from refrigerator and shape as directed; it may take slightly longer to rise. Bake as directed.

Sourdough Cornmeal Bread

The addition of cornmeal gives these golden free-form loaves a crunchy texture and an intriguing nutty flavor. *(Photograph on page 51.)*

        1   package active dry yeast
        2   cups warm water (about 110°)
       ¾   cup sourdough starter, at room
               temperature
       ¼   cup *each* salad oil and light molasses
        2   teaspoons salt
        2   cups yellow cornmeal
      6½ to 7 cups all-purpose flour, unsifted

In a large bowl, dissolve yeast in water. Add starter, oil, molasses, salt, and cornmeal; mix well. Gradually beat in enough of the flour (about 6 cups) to form a very stiff dough.

Turn dough out onto a floured board; knead until smooth (5 to 20 minutes), adding flour as needed to prevent sticking. Turn dough over in a greased bowl, cover and let rise in a warm place until doubled (about 1½ hours).

Punch dough down and divide in half. Knead each piece gently on a lightly floured board until it has a smooth surface. Shape each into a smooth round. Place loaves on lightly greased baking sheets; cover and let rise in a warm place until almost doubled (about 1½ hours).

Bake in a 375° oven for 30 to 35 minutes or until loaves turn a rich golden brown and sound hollow when tapped. Cool on racks. Makes 2 loaves.

Sour Rye Bread

Sourdough, combined with the bold flavors of rye and caraway, makes a deliciously tangy loaf to enjoy with cold meats and cheese. *(Photograph on page 51.)*

        2   cups warm water (about 110°)
        1   cup sourdough starter, at room
               temperature
        7   to 7½ cups all-purpose flour, unsifted
        2   cups rye flour, unsifted
        2   tablespoons light molasses
        2   teaspoons salt
        1   tablespoon caraway seeds
        1   teaspoon soda
            Cornmeal
            Boiling water
        1   teaspoon cornstarch mixed
               with ½ cup water

In a large bowl, stir together water, starter, and 4 cups of the all-purpose flour. Cover bowl with clear plastic wrap and let stand in a warm place until mixture is very bubbly and spongy-looking (about 6 to 8 hours).

Stir in rye flour, molasses, salt, caraway seeds, soda, and enough of the remaining all-purpose flour (about 1½ cups) to form a stiff dough.

Turn dough out onto a well-floured board; knead until smooth (15 to 20 minutes), adding flour as needed to prevent sticking. Turn dough over in a greased bowl; cover and let rise in a warm place until doubled (2 to 2½ hours).

Punch dough down and divide in half. Knead each piece gently on a lightly floured board just until dough has a smooth surface. If you have only 1 oven, wrap half the dough in clear plastic wrap and refrigerate.

For an oblong loaf, shape dough into a smooth log about 14 inches long. Sprinkle a piece of stiff cardboard (7 by 18 inches) with 3 tablespoons cornmeal and set loaf on top. For a round loaf, shape dough into a smooth ball. Place on a 12-inch-square piece of stiff cardboard sprinkled with 3 tablespoons cornmeal. Cover lightly and let rise in a warm place until puffy and almost doubled (1 to 1½ hours).

With oven racks in 2 lowest positions, place a baking sheet on top rack as oven preheats to 400°. Just before bread is ready to bake, place a rimmed baking sheet on lowest rack and pour in boiling water about ¼ inch deep.

Meanwhile, heat cornstarch and water to boiling, stirring; cool slightly. With a razor blade or sharp floured knife, cut ½-inch-deep slashes in top of loaf—3 slightly slanting slashes in oblong loaf, 4 slashes in a crisscross pattern in round loaf. Then brush top and sides evenly with cornstarch mixture. Carefully slide loaf from cardboard onto baking sheet in oven.

Bake at 400° for 10 minutes; then brush evenly again with cornstarch mixture. Bake for 20 to 25 minutes longer or until loaves are richly browned and sound hollow when tapped. Cool on racks. Makes 2 loaves.

When you put first loaf in oven, remove second piece of dough from refrigerator and shape as directed; it will take slightly longer to rise. Bake as directed.

Sourdough Potato Bread

These moist and tender round or braided loaves keep well for several days.

An electric mixer lets you take advantage of a short-cut mixing method. You combine the yeast with some of the flour and the other dry ingredients, add the potatoes and liquid, then beat well. Once most of the flour has been beaten into the mixture, little kneading is required. *(Photograph on page 51.)*

    1 package active dry yeast
 5½ to 6 cups all-purpose flour, unsifted
    ¼ cup sugar
    2 teaspoons salt
       Instant mashed potatoes (amount for 2
         servings) plus milk, butter, and salt as
         specified on box
    ¾ cup milk
    ¼ cup butter or margarine, melted and
         cooled
    2 eggs
    1 cup sourdough starter, at room
         temperature
    1 egg white beaten with 2 tablespoons
         water
       Poppy seeds (optional)

In large bowl of an electric mixer, combine yeast, 2 cups of the flour, sugar, and salt.

In a pan, prepare instant mashed potatoes according to package directions. Then stir in milk, butter, eggs, and starter; stir until blended.

Add potato mixture to dry ingredients and beat with mixer at medium speed for 2 minutes, scraping bowl occasionally. Add 1½ cups of the remaining flour and beat at medium speed for 2 minutes longer. With a heavy spoon, stir in enough of the remaining flour (about 1½ cups) to form a stiff dough.

Turn dough out onto a floured board; knead until smooth (5 to 20 minutes), adding flour as needed to prevent sticking. Turn dough over in a greased bowl; cover and let rise in a warm place until doubled (1½ to 2 hours).

Punch dough down; knead briefly on a lightly floured board to release air, and divide in half. For round loaves, shape each half into a smooth ball. For braided loaves, divide each half into thirds. Roll each piece to form a rope about 18 inches long. Place 3 ropes on a lightly greased baking sheet; pinch tops together and loosely braid. Pinch ends together and tuck underneath. Repeat for second loaf. Cover loaves and let rise in a warm place until almost doubled (about 45 minutes).

With a razor blade or sharp floured knife, cut ½-inch-deep slashes in tops of round loaves in a crisscross pattern. Brush loaves evenly with egg white mixture. Sprinkle braided loaves with poppy seeds, if desired.

Bake in a 350° oven for about 35 minutes or until loaves are richly browned and sound hollow when tapped. Cool on racks. Makes 2 large loaves.

Sourdough Whole Wheat Pan Bread

Yeast goes into this bread along with sourdough starter, making it rise a little faster. It has a chewy crust, hearty flavor, and light texture. *(Photograph on page 51.)*

    1 cup *each* milk and boiling water
    1 package active dry yeast
    3 cups whole wheat flour, unsifted
 4½ to 5 cups all-purpose flour, unsifted
    ¾ cup sourdough starter, at room
         temperature
    ¼ cup molasses
    1 tablespoon salt
    3 tablespoons butter or margarine, at room
         temperature
    1 teaspoon soda

In a large bowl, combine milk and boiling water; cool to about 110°, then add yeast; let stand 5 minutes to soften. Stir in whole wheat flour, 1 cup of the all-purpose flour, and starter; beat until smooth and elastic (about 5 minutes). Cover bowl with clear plastic wrap and let stand in a warm place until mixture is very bubbly and spongy-looking (about 1 hour).

Stir in molasses, salt, butter, and soda. Gradually mix in enough of the remaining flour (about 3 cups) to form a very stiff dough. Turn dough out onto a well-floured board and knead until smooth (10 to 20 minutes), adding flour as needed to prevent sticking. Turn dough over in a greased bowl; cover and let rise in a warm place until doubled (1 to 1½ hours).

Punch dough down, knead briefly on a lightly floured board to release air, and divide in half. Shape each half into a loaf, and place each in a well-greased 4½ by 8½-inch loaf pan. Cover and let rise in a warm place until almost doubled (35 to 45 minutes).

Bake in a 375° oven for about 35 minutes or until loaves are nicely browned and sound hollow when tapped. Turn out on racks to cool. Makes 2 loaves.

Left to right: Pan Dulce (page 60), Kulich (page 73), and Anise Bread (page 66).

Sweet Treats & Festive Fare

In this chapter you'll find a delectable array of yeast rolls, coffee cakes, and breads—all sweetened just enough to make them something very special. Many, with their rich fillings and glazes, spicy fragrances and elegant shapes, would make a festive centerpiece at a holiday buffet. Others in this selection of sweet treats will add gaiety to the breakfast table or irresistible temptation to brunch. Or, for the round-the-clock sweet tooth, serve them for tea and late evening snacks.

Buttermilk-Wheat Rolls

Breakfast sweet rolls take on extra flavor and wholesomeness when made with whole grain flour. And they'll be light and tender as well, with this sweet-dough recipe. Use the dough to make date-filled cres-

cents, upside-down buns, or filled swirls. You can try two of the flavors with each batch of dough.

- 1 package active dry yeast
- ¼ cup warm water (about 110°)
- 1¾ cups buttermilk, at room temperature
- 2 eggs, lightly beaten
- ⅓ cup firmly packed brown sugar
- 1½ teaspoons salt
- ¼ cup butter or margarine, melted and cooled
- 3 cups whole wheat flour, unsifted
- 3½ to 4 cups all-purpose flour, unsifted

In a large bowl, dissolve yeast in water. Add buttermilk, eggs, brown sugar, salt, and butter. Gradually add whole wheat flour and 1 cup of the all-purpose flour; beat for 5 minutes. Then gradually mix in enough of the remaining all-purpose flour (about 2 cups) to make a stiff dough. Turn out onto a floured board; knead until smooth and satiny (10 to 20 minutes), adding flour as needed to prevent sticking. Turn dough over in a greased bowl; cover and let rise in a warm place until doubled (about 2 hours).

Punch dough down; knead briefly on a lightly floured board to release air. Divide in half, shaping each half into a ball. Keep 1 ball covered while shaping the first in any of the ways suggested below. Bake as directed for each.

Upside-down Nut Buns

For topping, melt ¼ cup **butter** or margarine in a 9 by 13-inch baking pan; brush some of the butter over pan sides. Put ⅔ cup packed **brown sugar** and 3 tablespoons **light corn syrup** into pan; stir to blend, then spread evenly over pan bottom. Sprinkle about 1 cup **walnut or pecan** pieces over sugar mixture; set pan aside.

On a lightly floured board, roll out a half batch of Buttermilk-Wheat dough (facing page) into a 9 by 18-inch rectangle. Brush with 2 tablespoons melted **butter** or margarine, then sprinkle with ½ cup firmly packed **brown sugar** and 2 teaspoons **ground cinnamon.**

Starting with a wide side, roll up tightly jelly-roll fashion. Cut into 18 equal slices and set each, cut side down, in prepared pan. Cover lightly and let rise in a warm place until almost doubled (about 45 minutes). Bake in a 375° oven for 25 to 30 minutes or until well browned.

Remove from oven and invert pan onto a large tray. Wait 1 minute, then lift off pan, allowing syrup to drizzle over rolls. Makes 18 buns.

Apple-and-Prune Swirls

For filling, finely chop 1 medium-size peeled **Golden Delicious apple** to make 1 cup. Also finely chop pitted moist-pack **prunes** to make ½ cup. In a bowl, combine apple, prunes, ½ teaspoon grated **lemon peel,** ⅓ cup toasted chopped **almonds or walnuts,** 1 teaspoon **ground cinnamon,** ¼ teaspoon **ground nutmeg,** and 1 tablespoon **flour**; mix until well blended.

On a lightly floured board, roll out a half batch of Buttermilk-Wheat dough (facing page) into a 9 by 18-inch rectangle. Brush with 2 tablespoons melted **butter** or margarine, distribute ½ cup firmly packed **brown sugar** over dough, then scatter fruit mixture over top.

Starting with a long side, roll up tightly jelly-roll fashion. Cut into 18 equal slices and set each, cut side down, into a well-greased 2½-inch muffin cup. Cover lightly and let rise in a warm place until almost

doubled (about 45 minutes). Bake in a 375° oven for 18 to 20 minutes or until well browned.

For glaze, blend ½ cup unsifted **powdered sugar** with 1 tablespoon **water** and ¼ teaspoon **ground cinnamon.** Brush over buns while they're still hot. (If making rolls ahead, cool completely, freeze, and glaze after reheating.) Let buns cool slightly, then remove from pans. Makes 18.

Date-filled Crescents

For date filling, combine in a bowl ¾ cup *each* finely chopped pitted **dates** and **nuts** (walnuts, almonds, or pecans), 1 teaspoon grated **lemon peel,** and 1 tablespoon **lemon juice.** Shape into a rope, then divide into 24 equal parts. Also melt 5 tablespoons **butter** or margarine.

Divide a half batch of Buttermilk-Wheat dough (facing page) into 3 equal parts. Working with 1 part at a time (keep remainder covered), shape into a ball, roll on a floured board into a 10-inch circle, then brush with 1 tablespoon of the melted butter. Cut each circle into 8 wedges. For each bun, place a portion of filling near wide edge and roll toward point. Shape rolls into crescents and place, point down, about 1½ inches apart on greased baking sheets.

When all are formed, brush with remaining 2 tablespoons butter. Cover lightly and let rise in a warm place until almost doubled (30 to 40 minutes). Bake in a 400° oven for 15 to 18 minutes or until golden brown. Makes 24.

For nut glaze, blend in a bowl 1 cup unsifted **powdered sugar,** 1 tablespoon *each* **lemon juice** and **water,** and ¼ cup finely chopped **nuts.** While buns are hot or after they're reheated, brush tops with nut glaze.

Giant Upside-down Pecan Rolls

Each of these sweet pecan rolls is so generously proportioned that just one or two will feed a small family.

- ⅔ cup milk
- 1¾ cups sugar
- 1 teaspoon salt
- ½ cup butter or margarine
- 2 packages active dry yeast
- ½ cup warm water (about 110°)
- 5½ to 6 cups all-purpose flour, unsifted
- 2 eggs
- ¼ cup butter or margarine, melted
- 1 tablespoon ground cinnamon
- 1 cup coarsely chopped pecans
    Water
    Brown sugar-nut syrup (recipe follows)

(Continued on next page)

In a pan, combine milk, ¾ cup of the sugar, salt, and the ½ cup butter (cut in pieces). Heat, stirring, to about 110° (butter need not melt completely).

In a large bowl, dissolve yeast in water. Blend in milk mixture. Gradually mix in 3 cups of the flour, then beat for 5 minutes. Beat in 1 whole egg and 1 egg yolk (reserve remaining egg white), then gradually beat in enough of the remaining flour (about 2 cups) to make a stiff dough.

Turn dough out onto floured board; knead until smooth and satiny (10 to 20 minutes), adding flour as needed to prevent sticking. Turn dough over in a greased bowl; cover and let rise in a warm place until doubled (about 2 hours).

Punch dough down. Knead briefly on a lightly floured board to release air; let rest for 10 minutes. Then roll and stretch dough into a 24 by 18-inch rectangle. Brush evenly with the ¼ cup melted butter.

Combine the remaining 1 cup sugar with cinnamon; sprinkle evenly over butter, then sprinkle with pecans. Starting with a narrow side, roll up jelly-roll fashion. Moisten edge of dough with water and pinch it snugly against roll to seal. With a sharp knife, cut roll into 6 equal parts. Prepare brown sugar nut syrup, pour into pan, and arrange slices cut side up in pan. Cover; let rise in a warm place until almost doubled (about 1½ hours).

Brush surfaces of rolls with reserved egg white beaten with 1 teaspoon water. Bake, uncovered, in a 350° oven for 30 to 35 minutes or until well browned. Immediately invert onto a serving tray. Makes 6 large rolls, about 12 servings.

Brown sugar-nut syrup. Boil together ¼ cup **butter** or margarine, 2 tablespoons **water**, and 1 cup firmly packed **dark brown sugar** for 1 minute. Immediately pour into a 9 by 13-inch baking pan; tilt pan so syrup forms an even layer. Arrange 1 cup **pecan** halves, flat side up, on syrup.

Giant Cinnamon Rolls

Following recipe for Giant Pecan Rolls (page 57), prepare dough, roll out, and spread with the melted butter and cinnamon and sugar mixture. Instead of chopped nuts, use ½ to 1 cup **currants** or raisins. Roll and cut as directed. Omit brown sugar-nut syrup and arrange sections, cut side up, in a well-greased 9 by 13-inch baking pan; cover and let rise in a warm place until almost doubled (about 1½ hours).

Brush rolls with reserved egg white beaten with 1 teaspoon water. Bake, uncovered, in a 350° oven for 30 to 35 minutes or until well browned.

With a large spatula, transfer rolls from pan to racks. If they are to be served at once, drizzle with powdered sugar glaze (recipe follows) while still warm. (Or to store rolls for later use, leave plain, cool,

Icing isn't essential, of course ... but it does make Giant Cinnamon Rolls (recipe below left) even more tempting.

wrap, and freeze; glaze after reheating.) Makes 6 large rolls, about 12 servings. (*Photograph on facing page.*)

Powdered sugar glaze. Beat together until smooth 1½ cups unsifted **powdered sugar**, 1 tablespoon **butter** or margarine (at room temperature), ⅛ teaspoon **vanilla**, and 2 to 3 tablespoons warm **water**.

Honey Almond Buns

For a special occasion brunch or family breakfast, these fragrant buns with their golden honey-nut glaze make a delicious treat, either freshly baked or reheated.

  1 **package active dry yeast**
  ¼ **cup warm water (about 110°)**
  ¼ **cup honey**
  ½ **cup milk**
  ¼ **cup butter or margarine, melted and cooled**
  2 **eggs, slightly beaten**
  ½ **teaspoon salt**
  3½ **to 4 cups all-purpose flour, unsifted**
   Almond filling (recipe follows)

In a large bowl, dissolve yeast in water; stir in honey, milk, butter, eggs, and salt. Gradually add 3½ cups of the flour, mixing until well blended (dough will be sticky). Turn over in a greased bowl; cover and let rise in a warm place until doubled (about 1½ hours).

Turn dough out onto a floured board; knead until smooth and satiny (5 to 20 minutes), adding flour as needed to prevent sticking. Shape dough into a ball, pat down, and roll out into a 12 by 18-inch rectangle; spread almond filling evenly over dough. Starting with a long side, roll up jelly-roll fashion; cut into 1-inch slices and arrange cut side up in a well-greased 9 by 13-inch baking pan. Cover and let rise in a warm place until almost doubled (about 45 minutes).

Bake in a 350° oven for 35 minutes or until buns are well browned. Immediately invert onto plate or serving board; quickly scrape out any syrup left in pan and spread it over buns. Makes 1½ dozen buns.

Almond filling. Beat together ½ cup *each* **butter** or margarine (at room temperature), firmly packed **brown sugar**, and **honey** until blended. Stir in ½ cup *each* all-purpose **flour**, sliced **almonds**, and shredded **coconut**; 1 teaspoon **almond extract**; and ½ teaspoon **orange extract**.

Pan Dulce

Like other Mexican artisans, south-of-the-border bakers have a talent for creating fanciful designs. In their hands, a simple ball of dough plus some sweet crumb topping can become a seashell, a horn, or some other imaginatively shaped treat. All of these egg-rich yeast buns are called *pan dulce* (pahn *dool*-seh), which simply means sweet bread.

  1 **cup milk**
  6 **tablespoons butter or margarine**
  1 **package active dry yeast**
  1 **teaspoon salt**
  ⅓ **cup sugar**
  5 **to 5½ cups all-purpose flour, unsifted**
  2 **eggs**
     Plain and chocolate egg streusel (recipes follow)
  1 **egg beaten with 2 tablespoons milk**

In a pan, heat milk and butter (cut in pieces) until very warm (120° to 130°; butter need not melt completely). In large bowl of an electric mixer, combine yeast, salt, sugar, and 2 cups of the flour. Pour in milk mixture and beat on medium speed for 2 minutes, scraping bowl often. Blend in eggs and 1 cup more flour; beat on high speed for 2 minutes. Gradually beat in enough of the remaining flour (about 1½ cups) to form a stiff dough, using a wooden spoon or a heavy-duty mixer on low to medium speed.

Turn dough out onto floured board; knead until smooth and satiny (5 to 20 minutes), adding flour as needed to prevent sticking. Turn dough over in a greased bowl; cover and let rise in a warm place until doubled (about 1½ hours).

Prepare both plain and chocolate egg streusel mixtures.

Punch dough down and turn out onto floured board. Divide into 14 equal pieces and shape each into a smooth ball; then shape buns as shown below, making 7 round buns (shells) and 7 long shapes (horns and corns). Lightly pack streusel into cup or spoon when measuring amount indicated; for shells, squeeze streusel firmly into a ball, then either roll out smooth or break into lumps.

Place buns about 2 inches apart on greased baking sheets, placing streusel-topped buns on 1 sheet and filled buns on another; lightly cover filled buns only. Let buns rise in a warm place until almost doubled (about 45 minutes).

Brush filled buns with egg mixture.

Bake in a 375° oven for 17 to 20 minutes or until tops are lightly browned. Makes 14.

Plain egg streusel. In a bowl, mix ½ cup **sugar** with ⅔ cup unsifted **flour**. Cut in 3½ tablespoons **butter** or margarine with a pastry blender or by rubbing mixture between your fingers until fine, even crumbs form. With a fork, stir in 2 **egg yolks** until well blended.

Chocolate egg streusel. Prepare as for plain egg streusel, but add 2 tablespoons ground **chocolate** with the sugar and flour.

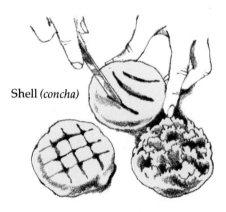

Shell *(concha)*

To make shell *(above)*, pat dough into 3-inch rounds; top with ¼ cup streusel either rolled to a smooth layer and slashed or piled in lumps. To make horn *(center)*, roll to 4 by 8-inch oval; top with 3 tablespoons streusel. Roll from one end; stop halfway and fold in sides; finish rolling and curl ends. To make corn *(far right)* proceed as for horn, but roll from one end to other, pulling ends out; slash top.

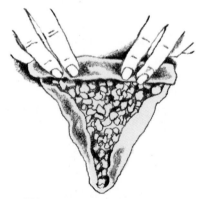

Horn *(cuerno)*

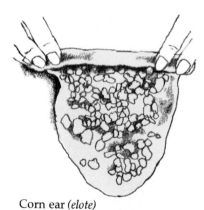

Corn ear *(elote)*

Bread Sculpture

A great big loaf designed to create a great big smile—that can be the effect when you put a little whimsy into the shape of your bread. For instance, as a personalized gift, you might present a mermaid to a fisherman or a teddy bear to a family with a new baby. Or, for a fanciful Easter treat, why not serve a fat, fragrant hen complete with golden egg? All three sculpture possibilities are shown on page 62.

The golden dough recipe offered here is enough for one large (about 2-pound) loaf. In deciding on your design, choose a form that you can put together with simple geometric shapes—ropes, rounds, ovals, and oblongs of dough. Keep the outline bold, the detail simple. For a maximum-size sculpture, you'll need to overlap two rimless baking sheets, adjusting them to fit your oven (leave a 1-inch space all around for heat circulation). Wrap them with foil. It might help to draw a full-size pattern on a sheet of paper that fits the overlapped sheets.

Golden Sculpture Dough

- 1 package active dry yeast
- ¼ cup warm water (about 110°)
- ¾ cup butter or margarine at room temperature
- ½ cup sugar
- ⅓ cup warm milk (about 110°)
- ½ teaspoon salt
- 5 eggs
- 5 to 5½ cups all-purpose flour, unsifted
- 1 egg beaten with 1 tablespoon water

In a large bowl, dissolve yeast in water. Stir in butter, sugar, milk, salt, and eggs until thoroughly blended. Gradually beat in about 4¾ cups of the flour to make a stiff dough—do not knead. Cover and let dough rise until doubled (about 1½ hours).

Beat down to release air; then knead on a lightly floured board until smooth and satiny (10 to 20 minutes), adding flour as needed to prevent sticking.

Divide dough into portions to fit your design, saving a small piece for decorative detail. Build sculpture on the greased, foil-covered, overlapped baking sheets.

For a solid area, shape dough into a ball and place smooth side up on the foil; then pat or roll out to achieve desired dimension and form (make no thicker than about 1 inch, or bread may crack during baking). Because dough expands as it rises and bakes, keep shapes about half as plump as you want them to be in the end.

Butt pieces of dough close together if they are to be joined. Leave at least 2 inches of space between parts you don't want to join. To attach small, round details (such as eyes), shape them into teardrops and set, points down, into holes poked into background dough. To create surface detail, such as mermaid's scales, or to separate areas like fingers or feathers, snip dough with scissors. Roll pieces of dough between your hands to make strands for arms, legs, or hair (try twisting, curling, or braiding strands).

Cover sculpture lightly and let rise in a warm place until puffy (about 30 minutes). Brush gently with egg mixture.

Bake in a 350° oven for about 30 minutes or until bread is richly browned and sounds hollow when tapped. Let cool on pan for 10 minutes; then slip a spatula beneath loaf and gently slide onto rack to cool completely. Makes 1 large loaf.

Portuguese Sweet Bread

This Portuguese sweet bread is rich with eggs and has a delicious lemony fragrance. The recipe makes one impressive golden loaf generous enough to serve a dozen guests. Because the dough is soft, it conforms well to the intricate curves and planes of a decorative mold. You can bake it in any fancy baking pan that holds about 2½ to 3 quarts, in a regular 10-inch tube pan, or even in a large salad mold.

If you prefer, you can make two smaller loaves, one to serve to the family right away and one to freeze. Or use the recipe to make 24 buns.

- 1 small baking potato, peeled and cut in thick slices
- 1½ cups boiling water
- 1 tablespoon milk
- 1 tablespoon butter or margarine
- 1 package active dry yeast
- ⅓ cup sweetened condensed milk
- ¾ cup sugar
- ¼ cup butter or margarine, melted and cooled
- 3 eggs, lightly beaten
- ½ teaspoon ground mace or nutmeg
- 1 teaspoon grated lemon peel
- 5 to 5½ cups all-purpose flour, unsifted

(Continued on page 63)

Whimsical loaves to gift wrap were made with Golden Sculpture Dough (see Bread Sculpture, page 61).

Fish-shaped Almond Loaves

You bake this golden bread from Switzerland in metal fish-shaped molds often used for gelatin salads. A core of rich almond filling runs through the bread, and sliced almonds make the scaly surface.

You can use the variation following this recipe to make the traditional Alsatian loaf called *kugelhof*. Baked in one large decorative tube pan, it has no filling. A dusting of powdered sugar highlights the surface pattern.

¾ **cup raisins**
1½ **tablespoons kirsch (cherry brandy) or**
   lemon juice
1 **package active dry yeast**
¼ **cup warm water (about 110°)**
½ **cup (¼ lb.) butter or margarine, at room**
   temperature
½ **cup sugar**
1 **teaspoon *each* grated lemon peel, vanilla,**
   and salt
3 **eggs**
3 **cups all-purpose flour, unsifted**
½ **cup milk**
   About 6 tablespoons sliced almonds
   Almond filling (recipe follows)
   Granulated or powdered sugar

Mix raisins with kirsch and set aside. In a small bowl, dissolve yeast in water. In a large bowl, beat butter with sugar, lemon peel, vanilla, and salt until well blended; then add eggs, one at a time, mixing thoroughly after each. Stir in yeast, then add flour alternately with milk, mixing well. Beat dough very well for 5 minutes. Mix in raisins and liqueur. Cover and let rise in a warm place until doubled (about 2 hours).

Meanwhile, generously butter 3 fish-shaped molds suitable for baking, *each* with 2½-cup capacity and about 10 inches long. In bottom of each pan, overlap sliced almonds like fish scales, starting just behind the head; you'll need about 2 tablespoons almonds for each mold.

Beat dough with a spoon to release air, then spoon about 1/6 of the dough into each mold; gently press out evenly with buttered fingers.

Lay a roll of almond filling into dough in each mold, pressing down gently so dough oozes up against filling. Spoon remaining dough equally into each mold, covering filling; with buttered fingers, press dough out to fill mold evenly and seal in filling. Cover molds and let rise until almost doubled (about 45 minutes).

Bake on lowest rack of a 350° oven for about 35 minutes or until loaves are well browned and sound hollow when tapped. Let cool in pans for about 10 minutes, then invert onto serving dish or racks. Sprinkle loaves with granulated or powdered sugar. Makes 3 small loaves; each serves 4.

(Continued on next page)

... Portuguese Sweet Bread (cont'd.)

Cook potato in boiling water until very soft (about 20 minutes). Drain, reserving ¾ cup cooking water; cool to 110°. Mash or beat potato until smooth, measure ½ cup, and add milk and the 1 tablespoon butter.

In a large bowl, dissolve yeast in cooled cooking water. Stir in condensed milk, sugar, melted butter, eggs, mace, lemon peel, and potato mixture.

Gradually beat in enough of the flour (about 4½ cups) to make a stiff dough. Turn dough out onto floured board; knead until smooth and satiny (5 to 20 minutes), adding flour as needed to prevent sticking. Turn dough over in a greased bowl; cover and let rise until doubled (about 45 minutes).

Punch dough down; knead briefly on a lightly floured board to release air. Shape and bake according to following directions to make 1 large loaf, 2 smaller loaves, or 24 buns.

For 1 large loaf, butter and dust with flour a 10-inch tube pan or a 2½- to 3-quart mold. For a tube pan, roll dough into a 16-inch-long rope and wind it into pan so that ends meet; pinch ends to seal. For a tubeless pan, shape dough into a ball with a smooth, rounded top and set smooth side down in pan. Cover and let rise until almost doubled (about 45 minutes). Bake in a 325° oven for about 50 minutes for tube pan, 60 minutes for tubeless pan, or until bread is well browned and begins to pull away from pan sides. Cool for 10 minutes in pan, then turn out on rack. If you wish, dust with powdered sugar before serving.

For 2 small loaves, butter two 9 by 5-inch loaf pans or 1½-quart molds and dust with flour. Divide dough in half and shape into loaves or balls; place in pans. Cover and let rise until almost doubled (about 30 minutes). Bake in a 325° oven for about 40 minutes or until bread is well browned and pulls away from pan sides. Cool as for large loaf.

For sweet bread buns, divide dough into 24 equal portions. Shape each portion into a smooth ball. Place balls about 3 inches apart on a lightly greased baking sheet. Or place each ball in a buttered and flour-dusted 2½-inch muffin cup. Cover and let rise until almost doubled (about 20 minutes). Bake in a 400° oven for 15 minutes or until browned. Cool on rack.

Showing respect for their staff of life, German bakers took care never to turn their backs to the oven. A Spanish custom, if a piece of bread drops to the floor, is to pick it up, kiss it, and place it on the table again to help a soul escape from purgatory.

Almond filling. Smoothly blend ¼ cup **butter** or margarine (at room temperature) and ⅔ cup unsifted **powdered sugar**. Add ⅓ cup unsifted flour and ½ cup **almond paste**; stir until crumbly and evenly mixed. Beat in 1 **egg white**. Cover and chill until easy to handle (about 30 minutes). Shape into 3 rolls, each about 8 inches long; cover and keep cold until ready to use.

Alsatian Kugelhof

Prepare dough as directed for Fish-shaped Almond Loaves (preceding), adding ⅓ cup coarsely chopped blanched **almonds** to dough along with raisins. Generously butter a 10-cup decorative tube pan mold and arrange only ¼ cup of the sliced almonds in bottom. After dough has risen once, stir down and pour into prepared pan. Omit almond filling. Cover and let rise in a warm place until dough almost reaches top of pan (about 1 hour).

Bake on lowest rack in a 350° oven for about 40 minutes or until loaf is well browned and sounds hollow when tapped. Let cool in pan for about 15 minutes; invert onto dish or rack to cool. Sprinkle with granulated or powdered **sugar**. Makes 1 loaf.

Almond-crusted Flat Bread

A chunky topping of almond paste and sliced almonds crowns these round, flat loaves. Beneath the crust is a moderately sweet, rich bread that's lightly flavored with orange and anise. Raisins and bits of candied orange peel lace the golden interior.

  1 **package active dry yeast**
  ¼ **cup warm water** (about 110°)
  ¾ **cup butter** or margarine, at room
      temperature
  ¾ **cup sugar**
  ⅓ **cup milk**
  ½ **teaspoon salt**
  1 **tablespoon** *each* **grated orange peel** and
      anise seed
  4 **eggs**
  1 **egg yolk**
4¾ to 5 **cups all-purpose flour**, unsifted
  1 **cup raisins**
  1 **cup diced candied orange peel**
  1 **egg white** beaten with 1 tablespoon water
      About 7 ounces **almond paste**
  1 **cup sliced almonds**
      Powdered sugar

In large bowl of an electric mixer, dissolve yeast in water. Add butter, sugar, milk, salt, grated orange peel, anise seed, eggs, and egg yolk. Mix to blend well.

With electric mixer on medium speed, gradually add 2 cups of the flour and beat for 10 minutes. Mix in 1 cup of the remaining flour with mixer at low speed, or with a wooden spoon, until thoroughly moistened. Then stir in 1¾ cups of the remaining flour with a spoon (or heavy-duty mixer), moistening thoroughly (do not knead).

Cover bowl and let dough rise in a warm place until doubled (1½ to 2 hours). Beat to release air, then turn out on a well-floured board.

Knead until smooth and satiny (about 10 minutes), adding as little flour as possible. Flatten dough and place raisins and candied orange peel on top. Fold dough over and knead lightly just until fruit is well distributed.

Divide dough into 2 equal parts and shape each into a ball. Place each on a well-greased baking sheet and pat into a flat round about 9 inches in diameter. Cover lightly and set in a warm place until puffy-looking (40 to 45 minutes). Brush with egg white mixture. Crumble almond paste into about ½-inch chunks and sprinkle half over each round; then sprinkle half of the almonds over each. Press lightly into dough.

Place pans on middle rack of a 350° oven (or stagger pans on 2 racks closest to middle of oven; racks should be at least 4 inches apart) and bake for about 30 minutes or until bread is richly browned. With a spatula, transfer breads to racks to cool. To serve, dust generously with powdered sugar. Makes 2 loaves.

Heart or Butterfly Coffee Cake

Buttery Danish coffee cake, warm and fragrant from your oven, makes a special breakfast treat almost any way you shape it. But with just a few extra steps—rolling, folding, slashing, and twisting—you can turn this oversize coffee cake into a big fanciful butterfly or heart shape to add to the pleasure of making and serving it.

You can fill the coffee cake with traditional cinnamon-sugar and nuts. Or, for variety, try Danish-style frangipane filling made with almond paste, or tangy apricot-nut filling.

  1/3 cup milk
   3 tablespoons sugar
  1/2 teaspoon salt
  1/4 cup butter or margarine
   1 package active dry yeast
  1/4 cup warm water (about 110°)
   3 to 3 1/2 cups all-purpose flour, unsifted
   2 eggs
  1/2 teaspoon almond extract
   1 teaspoon grated lemon peel
     Cinnamon-nut, frangipane, or apricot-nut
       filling (recipes follow)

In a pan, combine milk, sugar, salt, and butter (cut in pieces). Heat, stirring, to about 110° (butter need not melt completely). In a large bowl, dissolve yeast in water; blend in milk mixture. Add 1 1/2 cups of the flour and stir to moisten evenly. Beat in eggs, almond extract, and lemon peel until smoothly blended. Then stir in 1 cup of the remaining flour.

Turn dough out onto floured board; knead until smooth and satiny (5 to 20 minutes), adding flour as needed to prevent sticking. Turn dough over in a greased bowl; cover and let rise until doubled (about 1 1/2 hours).

Punch dough down, knead briefly on lightly floured board to release air, and roll into a 12 by 18-inch rectangle. Cover with your choice of fillings to within 1 inch of edges.

Starting with a long side, roll up jelly-roll fashion; pinch seam along top to seal. Then fold the roll, tightly pinch ends together, and tuck them under. Place on a large, lightly greased baking sheet and slash and shape the roll for either the butterfly or heart, as shown below.

Cover lightly and let rise until almost doubled (about 45 minutes). Bake in a 350° oven for 25 minutes or until golden brown. Makes 1 large coffee cake.

Cinnamon-nut filling. Brush dough rectangle with 3 tablespoons melted **butter** or margarine. Combine 1/4 cup *each* **granulated sugar** and firmly packed **brown sugar** and 1 1/2 teaspoons **ground cinnamon**; distribute evenly over buttered area of dough as directed; sprinkle with 3/4 cup sliced **almonds**.

Frangipane (almond paste) filling. In small bowl of an electric mixer, beat 4 tablespoons **butter** or margarine (at room temperature) until creamy. Gradually add 1 can (8 oz.) **almond paste**, 1/2 cup unsifted **powdered sugar**, 1 **egg**, and 1/2 teaspoon grated **lemon peel**; continue beating until well blended and smooth. Spread over dough rectangle as directed; sprinkle with 3/4 cup sliced **almonds**.

Apricot-nut filling. In a small pan, combine 1 cup moist-pack dried **apricots**, chopped; 1/2 cup **raisins**; and 1/4 cup *each* **water** and **sugar**. Cover; simmer, stirring occasionally, until mixture is soft and thick (about 10 minutes). Spread over dough as directed; sprinkle with 1/2 cup chopped **pecans or walnuts**.

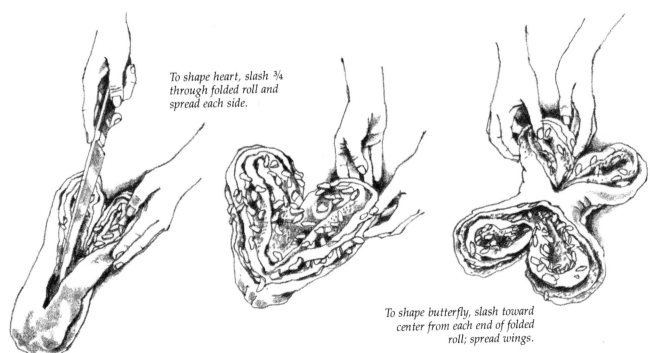

To shape heart, slash 3/4 through folded roll and spread each side.

To shape butterfly, slash toward center from each end of folded roll; spread wings.

Anise Bread

Festive breads to grace a Christmas buffet (left to right): Russian Krendl and Belgian Cramique (both on page 69), and Swedish Cardamom Wreath (page 71).

For festive occasions in northeastern New Mexico, it's a tradition to bake a sweet yeast bread with the flavor of anise. Serve this tender treat warm or toasted to enhance its spicy fragrance.

  1 **package active dry yeast**
 ½ **cup warm water (about 110°)**
 ½ **cup warm milk (about 110°)**
  2 **tablespoons sugar**
1½ **tablespoons anise seeds**
 ½ **cup (¼ lb.) butter or margarine, melted and cooled**
  2 **eggs**
 ½ **teaspoon salt**
4½ **to 5 cups all-purpose flour, unsifted**
 ⅔ **cup firmly packed brown sugar mixed with ½ teaspoon ground cinnamon**
     Sugar glaze (recipe follows)

In a large bowl, dissolve yeast in water. Add milk, sugar, anise seeds, 3 tablespoons of the butter, eggs, salt, and 1½ cups of the flour. Beat for about 5 minutes, then gradually beat in about 2½ cups more flour to make a soft dough.

Turn dough out onto floured board; knead until smooth and satiny (5 to 20 minutes), adding flour as needed to prevent sticking. Turn dough over in a greased bowl; cover and let rise in a warm place until doubled (about 1½ hours). Punch dough down, knead briefly on lightly floured board to release air, and roll out into a 12 by 22-inch rectangle. Brush remaining 5 tablespoons butter over dough to within ½ inch of edges. Sprinkle brown sugar-cinnamon mixture evenly over butter. Starting with a wide side, roll up tightly jelly-roll fashion, pinching edge to seal.

Being careful not to stretch roll, place it seam side down in a greased 10-inch tube pan; pinch ends together to close circle. With a razor blade or sharp floured knife, make 7 evenly spaced slashes, ½ inch deep, on top. Cover and let rise in a warm place until almost doubled (about 45 minutes).

Bake in a 350° oven for 50 to 60 minutes or until loaf is lightly browned and sounds hollow when tapped. Cool in pan 5 minutes; then turn out on rack. While still warm, spoon on sugar glaze, letting it drizzle down sides. (If made ahead, let bread cool completely and freeze; glaze after reheating.) Makes 1 loaf.

Sugar glaze. Blend ½ cup unsifted **powdered sugar** with 1 tablespoon **water** until smooth.

Potica

In Yugoslavia, the fall harvest of nuts signals the time to bake this rich, lavishly nut-filled coffee bread (pronounced poh-*tee*-tsa). Our recipe treats it as a batter bread—you spoon alternate layers of dough and ground nut filling into two large ring molds or tube pans. The fine-grained loaves that result have a honey and cinnamon-flavored walnut filling that compactly rings their interior.

  2 **packages active dry yeast**
 ½ **cup warm water (about 110°)**
1½ **cups warm milk (about 110°)**
 ¾ **cup butter or margarine, melted and cooled**
 ½ **cup sugar**
  2 **teaspoons** *each* **salt and grated lemon peel**
  2 **eggs**
  5 **cups all-purpose flour, unsifted**
     Walnut filling (recipe follows)
     Powdered sugar

In a large bowl, dissolve yeast in water. Add milk, butter, sugar, salt, lemon peel, and eggs; mix to blend well. Beat in flour, 1 cup at a time, beating well after each addition, to make an elastic dough.

Cover bowl and let dough rise in a warm place until doubled (about 1 hour). Beat down; spoon about ¼ of dough into each of 2 well-greased 10-cup plain or fancy tube pans or ring molds, spreading in thin, even layers. Spoon ½ the filling in an even ring over dough in each pan; filling should not touch pan sides or center tube. Top each with ½ the remaining dough, smoothing it over filling and against pan sides. Cover and let rise until puffy (about 20 minutes).

Bake in a 350° oven for about 45 minutes or until golden brown. Cool in pans for 5 minutes; then turn out on racks. Dust with powdered sugar just before serving. Serve warm or reheated. Makes 2 loaves.

Walnut filling. In a blender, whirl 2¾ cups (about ¾ lb.) **walnuts**, about ¼ at a time, until finely ground. In a pan, bring ⅓ cup **half-and-half** (light cream) to simmering, then stir into nuts in a bowl. Gradually stir in ¼ cup **sugar**, 2 teaspoons **ground cinnamon**, 1 tablespoon **vanilla**, and ½ cup **honey**. Separate 1 **egg** and stir yolk into nut mixture. Beat white until stiff peaks form; fold into nut mixture.

Poppy Seed Coffee Cake

Bakers throughout eastern Europe are famous for their artistry with poppy seeds in cakes and breads. This breakfast loaf is one delicious example. The slate-colored seeds contribute an intriguing nutlike flavor and crunchy texture.

Because of the large amount of poppy seeds required, you may want to buy a half pound (about 1½ cups) at a health food store. Or check stores that specialize in spices, coffee, and nuts.

> 1 **package active dry yeast**
> ¼ **cup warm water (about 110°)**
> ¼ **cup warm milk (about 110°)**
> ½ **teaspoon salt**
> ¼ **cup sugar**
> 1 **egg**
> ¼ **cup butter or margarine, at room temperature**
> 3 to 3½ **cups all-purpose flour, unsifted**
>   **Poppy seed filling (recipe follows)**
> 1 **egg white beaten with 1 teaspoon water**
> 2 **tablespoons sliced almonds**

In a large bowl, dissolve yeast in water. Blend in milk, salt, sugar, egg, and butter. Gradually beat in about 2½ cups of the flour to make a soft dough.

Turn dough out onto a floured board; knead until smooth and satiny (5 to 20 minutes), adding flour as needed to prevent sticking. Turn dough over in a greased bowl; cover and let rise in a warm place until doubled (1 to 1½ hours).

Punch dough down; turn out onto lightly floured board and roll into a 10 by 15-inch rectangle. Place on a lightly greased baking sheet; mark dough lightly into 3 lengthwise sections. Spread filling in center ⅓ of dough. With a sharp knife, cut 10 diagonal strips in each of the 2 outer sections of dough, cutting in almost as far as the filling. As shown below, overlap strips: first one from left side, then one from right, alternating until all strips are folded over.

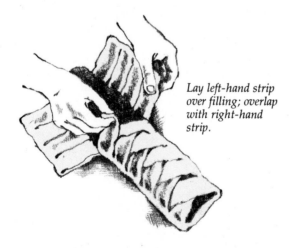

Lay left-hand strip over filling; overlap with right-hand strip.

Brush loaf with egg white mixture and sprinkle almonds evenly over top. Let rise, uncovered, in a warm place until almost doubled (about 30 minutes). Bake in a 350° oven for about 30 minutes or until richly browned. Cool on rack. Makes 1 large loaf.

Poppy seed filling. In a blender, combine ¾ cup **poppy seeds** and ¾ cup blanched whole **almonds**; whirl until mixture is consistency of cornmeal. In a small pan, combine seed-nut mixture with ½ cup **sugar**, ⅓ cup **milk**, ¾ teaspoon grated **lemon peel**, 1 tablespoon **lemon juice**, and 3 tablespoons **butter** or margarine. Cook over low heat, stirring, until mixture boils and thickens (about 10 minutes). Cool.

Houska

This seeded, raisin-studded braid from Czechoslovakia is customarily served during the Christmas holiday. A plump loaf delicately flavored with lemon and nutmeg, it is slightly less sweet than many Christmas breads.

> 1 **package active dry yeast**
> ¼ **cup warm water (about 110°)**
> ⅓ **cup warm milk (about 110°)**
> ¼ **cup butter or margarine, melted and cooled**
> 2 **eggs**
> ⅓ **cup sugar**
> ½ **teaspoon salt**
> 1 **teaspoon grated lemon peel**
> ¼ **teaspoon ground nutmeg**
> 3 to 3½ **cups all-purpose flour, unsifted**
> ⅔ **cup raisins**
> 1 **egg white beaten with 1 tablespoon water**
> 1 **teaspoon poppy, sesame, or caraway seeds**

In a large bowl, dissolve yeast in water. Blend in milk, butter, eggs, sugar, salt, lemon peel, nutmeg, and 1½ cups of the flour. Beat very well for about 5 minutes, then stir in about 1¼ cups of the remaining flour and the raisins to form a stiff dough. Turn dough out onto a floured board; knead until smooth (about 5 minutes). Turn dough over in a greased bowl; cover and let rise in a warm place until doubled (about 1½ hours).

Punch dough down and divide into 4 equal portions. Roll each to form a rope about 21 inches long. Place ropes side by side diagonally across a greased baking sheet; pinch tops together and braid loosely as follows: pick up rope on right, bring it over next one, under the third, and over the fourth. Repeat, always starting with rope on right, until braid is complete. Tuck ends under and pinch to seal. Cover lightly and let rise until almost doubled (about 1 hour).

Brush loaf with egg white mixture; sprinkle with seeds. Bake in a 350° oven for about 30 minutes or until loaf is golden brown and sounds hollow when tapped. Cool on rack. Makes 1 loaf.

Russian Krendl

Traditionally served as a birthday treat in Russia, this festive apple, kumquat, and prune-filled bread would brighten any other special occasion as well. You might want to serve it on Christmas morning. (*Photograph on page 67.*)

    2 packages active dry yeast
  ½ cup warm water (about 110°)
 1¼ teaspoons salt
    3 tablespoons sugar
    2 teaspoons vanilla
    1 cup warm milk (about 110°)
    6 to 6½ cups all-purpose flour, unsifted
    6 egg yolks, slightly beaten
  ⅔ cup butter or margarine, melted and
       cooled
  ¼ cup sugar mixed with 1 teaspoon ground
       cinnamon
    Fruit filling (recipe follows)
    1 egg yolk beaten with 1 tablespoon water
    Sugar glaze (recipe follows)
  ¼ cup sliced almonds

In a large bowl, dissolve yeast in water. Stir in salt, sugar, vanilla, and milk. Beat in 2 cups of the flour to make a smooth batter. Blend in egg yolks and ½ cup of the butter, then beat in 3½ cups of the remaining flour to make a soft dough.

Turn dough out onto a floured board; knead until smooth and satiny (5 to 20 minutes), adding flour as needed to prevent sticking. Turn dough over in a greased bowl; cover and let rise in a warm place until doubled (about 45 minutes).

Punch dough down and divide in half. Roll each half into a 9 by 30-inch rectangle. Brush each rectangle with half the remaining melted butter, then sprinkle with half the cinnamon-sugar and half the fruit filling. Starting with a long side, roll up jelly-roll fashion; moisten edge with water and pinch to seal. Place each roll, seam side down, on a greased baking sheet. Shape roll as shown at right; flatten slightly. Cover and let rise until almost doubled (about 45 minutes).

Brush loaves with egg yolk mixture. Bake in a 350° oven for about 45 minutes or until loaves are richly browned and sound hollow when tapped. Let cool on racks for 20 minutes, then brush each with half the glaze and top with sliced almonds. (If made ahead, let cool completely, freeze, and glaze after bread has been reheated.) Makes 2 loaves.

Fruit filling. Chop enough seeded canned **kumquats** to make ⅔ cup and combine with 1 cup *each* chopped pitted moist-pack **prunes** and chopped dried **apple slices**.

Sugar glaze. Beat together until smooth 1 tablespoon melted **butter** or margarine, 2 tablespoons hot **water**, 1½ cups sifted **powdered sugar**, and ¼ teaspoon grated **lemon peel**.

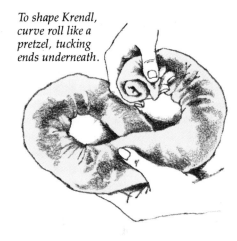

To shape Krendl, curve roll like a pretzel, tucking ends underneath.

Belgian Cramique

This egg-rich raisin bread with its glossy, golden crust is so beautiful you might like to serve it at Christmas or give it as a gift. It owes its festive shape to a wreath of topknotted brioche rolls. (*Photograph on page 67.*)

    1 cup milk
  ¼ cup butter or margarine
  ⅓ cup sugar
    1 teaspoon salt
    2 packages active dry yeast
  ½ cup warm water (about 110°)
    3 eggs
 5½ to 6 cups all-purpose flour, unsifted
    1 cup seedless raisins
    1 egg yolk beaten with 1 tablespoon water

In a pan, combine milk, butter (cut in pieces), sugar, and salt. Heat, stirring, to about 110° (butter need not melt completely). Dissolve yeast in warm water, then stir yeast and eggs into milk mixture. Gradually beat in 5 cups of the flour to make a soft dough.

Add raisins and turn dough out onto a floured board; knead until smooth and satiny (5 to 20 minutes), adding flour as needed to prevent sticking. Turn dough over in a greased bowl; cover and let rise in a warm place until doubled (about 45 minutes).

Punch dough down, knead briefly, then divide into 12 equal parts. Pinch off about 1/5 of each part and set aside to shape topknots. Shape each larger piece into a smooth ball; place smooth side up around outside edges of 2 greased 9-inch cake pans (each pan will hold 6 balls). Shape each smaller piece into a teardrop that is smooth on top. With your finger, poke a hole in center of each large ball and insert pointed end of tear drop in hole—settle securely or it may pop off at an angle while baking. Cover and let rise in a warm place until almost doubled (about 45 minutes).

Brush loaves with egg yolk mixture, being careful not to let it accumulate in joints of topknots. Bake in a 350° oven for about 45 minutes or until richly browned. Let cool in pans for 5 minutes, then turn out on racks. Makes 2 loaves.

Snowy white, filled Nut Stollen (recipe below) makes a delicious gift to sample on Christmas morning.

Nut Stollen

Stollen, originally a German Christmas bread with many variations, is most commonly shaped as a folded oval—like a giant Parker House roll. Traditionally, nuts and candied fruits are laced throughout the bread, but we find that folding the dough creates an ideal pocket for a toasty nut filling. (*Photograph on facing page.*)

    1 package active dry yeast
    ¼ cup warm water (about 110°)
    6 tablespoons sugar
    ¼ teaspoon salt
    ½ cup warm milk (about 110°)
    6 tablespoons butter, melted and cooled
    3 egg yolks
    3 to 3½ cups all-purpose flour, unsifted
       Nut filling (recipe follows)
    1 egg white, slightly beaten
    1 cup unsifted powdered sugar blended
         with 4 teaspoons milk
       Whole or half nuts for decoration

In a large bowl, dissolve yeast in water. Stir in sugar, salt, milk, butter, and egg yolks; blend well. Gradually beat in about 2½ cups of the flour to make a soft dough. Turn dough out onto floured board; knead until smooth and satiny (5 to 20 minutes), adding flour as needed to prevent sticking. Turn dough over in a greased bowl; cover and let rise in a warm place until doubled (about 1½ hours).

Punch dough down, knead briefly on a lightly floured board to release air, and shape into a smooth ball. Roll out to make a 10 by 12-inch oval and place on a greased baking sheet. Mound nut filling on one half of the 12-inch length of dough; fold plain section over filling and pat gently in place. Lightly cover and let rise in a warm place until puffy (about 30 minutes). Brush with egg white.

Bake in a 325° oven for about 45 minutes or until well browned. Cool on rack. While still warm, glaze surface with powdered sugar mixture and decorate with nuts. (If made ahead, cool completely and freeze; glaze after bread is reheated.) Makes 1 loaf.

Nut filling. In a wide frying pan over medium heat, melt 1½ tablespoons **butter** or margarine. Add 1¼ cups **nuts** (whole or large pieces of almonds, blanched filberts, or walnuts) and cook, stirring, until nuts are toasted and pale gold in the center (break one to test). Add ¼ cup firmly packed **brown sugar** and ¼ teaspoon ground **cinnamon**; continue cooking over low heat, stirring, until sugar melts. Set mixture aside until cool; then whirl, a portion at a time, to a coarse powder in a covered blender (or put through a nut grater); blend with 2 to 3 tablespoons **apricot jam** or orange marmalade.

Swedish Cardamom Wreath

One of the pleasures of Christmas morning, perhaps after gifts have been opened, can be sharing a loaf of this warm and fragrant breakfast bread with your family.

Flavored with aromatic cardamom, our braided Swedish wreaths are decorated with icing and cherries. Since cutting tends to squash this tender bread, it's best to pull it apart to serve. (*Photograph on page 67.*)

    1   package active dry yeast
    ¼   cup warm water (about 110°)
    2½ cups warm milk (about 110°)
    ¾   cup butter or margarine, melted and
          cooled
    1   egg
    ½   teaspoon salt
    1   cup sugar
    1½ teaspoons ground cardamom
    7 to 7½ cups all-purpose flour, unsifted
        Sugar icing (recipe follows)
        Red or green candied cherries, halved
          (optional)

In a large bowl, dissolve yeast in water. Stir in milk, butter, egg, salt, sugar, and cardamom until blended.

Gradually beat in about 7 cups of the flour to make a stiff dough. Turn dough out onto a floured board; knead until smooth and satiny (10 to 20 minutes), adding flour as needed to prevent sticking. Turn dough over in a greased bowl; cover and let rise in a warm place until doubled (1½ to 2 hours).

Punch dough down and divide into 6 equal portions; roll each to form a rope about 24 inches long. Place 3 ropes on a greased baking sheet; pinch tops together and loosely braid. Curve braid to make a wreath, pinching ends together. Repeat to make second wreath. Cover and let rise in a warm place until almost doubled (about 40 minutes).

Bake in a 350° oven for 35 to 40 minutes or until medium brown. Cool on racks for 10 minutes. Spoon sugar icing over tops of wreaths, letting it drizzle down sides. Decorate with cherries if you wish. (If made ahead, cool completely and freeze; decorate with icing and cherries after bread is reheated.) Makes 2 large loaves.

Sugar icing. For each loaf, beat until smooth 1 cup unsifted **powdered sugar**, 2 tablespoons **milk**, and ½ teaspoon **lemon extract**. Double recipe to make icing for 2 loaves.

Christopomo

Decorated with a sculptured cross modeled from ropes of dough, this round Greek Christmas loaf is rich with eggs and pleasantly flavored with anise.

    2 packages active dry yeast
    ½ cup warm water (about 110°)
    ½ cup warm milk (about 110°)
    1 cup (½ lb.) butter or margarine, melted
        and cooled
    4 eggs, slightly beaten
    ¾ cup sugar
    2 teaspoons crushed anise seed
    1 teaspoon salt
    7 to 7½ cups all-purpose flour, unsifted
    9 candied cherries or walnut halves
    1 egg white beaten with 1 tablespoon water

In a large bowl, dissolve yeast in water. Blend in milk, butter, eggs, sugar, anise seed, and salt. Gradually beat in about 7 cups of the flour to make a stiff dough.

Turn dough out onto a floured board; knead until smooth and satiny (10 to 20 minutes), adding flour as needed to prevent sticking. Turn dough over in a greased bowl; cover and let rise in a warm place until doubled (about 2 hours).

Punch dough down; pinch off 2 balls of dough, each about 3 inches in diameter; set aside. Shape remaining dough into a smooth ball. Place on a greased baking sheet and flatten into a 10-inch round.

Gently roll each of the 3-inch balls between your hands to make a 15-inch-long rope. With a razor blade or a sharp floured knife, cut a 5-inch-long slash into each end of the 2 ropes. Cross ropes on center of loaf; *do not press down.* Curl slashed sections away from center of each rope as shown below; then place a candied cherry or walnut half in each curl and one in center of cross. Brush loaf with beaten egg white. Cover lightly and let rise in a warm place until almost doubled (about 1 hour).

Bake in a 350° oven for about 45 minutes or until loaf is richly browned and sounds hollow when tapped. Makes 1 large loaf.

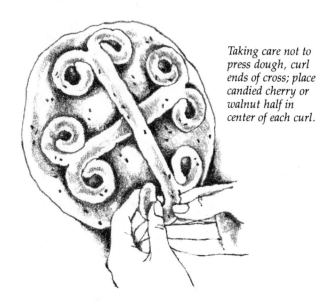

Taking care not to press dough, curl ends of cross; place candied cherry or walnut half in center of each curl.

Greek Easter Egg Braid

This festive braid called *tsoureki* (pronounced *too*-reki) wraps around colorful hard-cooked eggs. The Greeks favor bright red eggs—but because the dye seeps into the dough, you may prefer pastel shades that tinge it less. *(Photograph on page 75.)*

    ½ teaspoon salt
    ¼ cup sugar
    ¼ cup butter or margarine
    ½ cup milk
    2½ to 3 cups all-purpose flour, unsifted
    1 package active dry yeast
    2 eggs
    1 teaspoon vanilla
    1½ teaspoons grated lemon peel
    5 hard-cooked eggs, colored, at room
        temperature
    1 egg yolk beaten with 1 tablespoon water

In a pan combine salt, sugar, butter, and milk; warm over low heat to about 125°. In large bowl of an electric mixer, combine 1 cup of the flour with yeast. Add warm milk mixture, eggs, vanilla, and lemon peel. Beat at low speed, scraping bowl, until moistened. Then beat at high speed for 3 minutes (or beat by hand for 5 minutes). With a spoon, beat in enough of the remaining flour (about 1⅓ cups) to make a stiff dough.

Turn dough out onto a floured board; knead until smooth and elastic (10 to 20 minutes), adding flour as needed to prevent sticking. Turn dough over in a greased bowl; cover and let rise in a warm place until doubled (about 45 minutes).

Punch dough down, knead briefly on a lightly floured board to release air, and divide into 3 equal portions. Gently roll each with your hands to make a rope about 28 inches long. Place ropes side by side on a greased baking sheet; pinch tops together. Braid, then curve braid to form a ring, pinching ends together.

At evenly spaced intervals, press colored eggs upright between ropes of dough. Cover and let rise until almost doubled (about 30 minutes). Press eggs into dough again if necessary.

Brush egg yolk mixture evenly over braid without touching eggs. Bake in a 350° oven for 25 to 35 minutes or until bread is richly browned. Cool on rack. Makes 1 loaf.

Colomba di Pasqua

During the season when Easter and the coming of spring share festivities, breads take on special shapes and flavors in Italy. One very handsome loaf is shaped like its name—Easter dove, or *colomba di Pasqua* (pronounced *pah*-squaw). *(Photograph on page 75.)*

1 package active dry yeast
¼ cup warm water (about 110°)
½ cup butter or margarine, at room temperature
10 tablespoons (½ cup plus 2 tablespoons) sugar
2 tablespoons grated lemon peel
2 teaspoons vanilla
½ teaspoon salt
3 whole eggs
3 egg yolks
½ cup warm milk (about 110°)
5 to 5½ cups all-purpose flour, unsifted
About 4 ounces (4 to 5 tablespoons or half an 8-oz. can) almond paste
About 26 whole blanched almonds
1 egg white, slightly beaten
Sugar

In a small bowl, dissolve yeast in water. In a large bowl, beat together butter, sugar, lemon peel, vanilla, and salt until fluffy. Beat in eggs and egg yolks, 1 at a time. Mix in milk and dissolved yeast; then gradually beat in 4½ cups of the flour to make a soft dough.

Turn dough out onto a floured board; knead until smooth and satiny (10 to 20 minutes), adding flour as needed to prevent sticking. Turn dough over in a greased bowl; cover and let rise in a warm place until doubled (about 1½ hours).

Punch dough down; knead briefly on lightly floured board to release air. Divide in half and shape each half into a smooth ball. In center of a greased 14 by 17-inch baking sheet, flatten 1 dough ball and roll out across narrow dimension of pan to make an oval

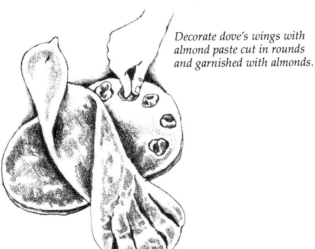

Decorate dove's wings with almond paste cut in rounds and garnished with almonds.

about 11 inches long and 6 inches wide. On a floured board, roll out other ball of dough to make a softly outlined triangle about 16 inches tall and 8 inches across the base. Lay triangle across oval as shown below. Fold over narrow end to make head; pinch firmly to form beak. Fold wide end in the opposite direction to make tail; gently pull tail into fan shape and cut into 5 strips to simulate feathers.

Pinch off 26 pieces of almond paste and press an almond into each; then press into wings. Let rise in a warm place until puffy (about 25 minutes). Brush gently with beaten egg white and sprinkle wings generously with sugar. Bake in a 350° oven for about 40 minutes or until bread is richly browned—cover with foil the last 15 minutes. Cool on rack. Makes 1 large loaf.

Kulich

The towering Russian Easter bread known as kulich always has a fresh white cap. You can top it with powdered sugar icing, a starched linen napkin, or a paper doily held in place with icing. A traditional crowning touch is to add a delicate rosebud, either fresh or made of frosting.

To achieve kulich's shape, you bake it in a juice can (46 fluid-ounce size); you'll need two cans for this recipe. To assure an exceptionally light and fluffy texture, our recipe suggests a rather unusual mixing method: you pull up handfuls of dough and rapidly hurl them back into the bowl until the dough comes up as one lump.

½ cup milk
1 cup (½ lb.) sweet butter, at room temperature
3½ cups all-purpose flour, unsifted
1 egg
1 package active dry yeast
¼ cup warm water (about 110°)
1 cup sugar
½ teaspoon salt
8 egg yolks
1 vanilla bean, 6 to 8 inches long
1 tablespoon vodka or brandy
Pinch of ground saffron (optional)
¼ cup finely chopped candied orange peel
Glaze and decorations (recipe follows)

In a small pan, combine ¼ cup of the milk and 2 tablespoons of the butter; bring to a boil, stirring. At once, dump in ¼ cup of the flour; remove from heat and stir vigorously until mixture is smooth and pulls from pan sides. Add egg and beat until thoroughly blended. Set mixture aside.

In a large bowl, dissolve yeast in warm water, then stir in 1 teaspoon of the sugar; let stand for about 5 minutes to soften. When cooked mixture is lukewarm, stir it into yeast mixture. Cover and let stand in a warm place until about doubled and very foamy (about 30 minutes).

In a separate bowl, beat remaining butter with salt and remaining sugar until blended; then beat in egg yolks, a few at a time.

Split vanilla bean lengthwise with a sharp knife; scrape out black seeds and mix them with vodka along with saffron (tuck empty pod into a jar of sugar to make vanilla-flavored sugar). Add vodka mixture to butter and sugar, then stir into yeast mixture. Mix in remaining flour alternately with remaining ¼ cup milk. Add orange peel.

With lightly oiled or buttered hands, rapidly pull handfuls of the very soft dough from bowl and forcefully throw dough back in, until it lifts as a whole lump, cleaning bowl fairly well as it comes up—takes about 45 minutes. (Or if you have a dough hook, beat until mixture begins to pull fairly cleanly from sides of bowl—about 30 minutes.)

Cover dough and let rise in a warm place until doubled (2 to 2½ hours).

Line bottoms of 2 juice cans with wax paper, heavily buttered and dusted with flour. Then line sides of cans with buttered and flour-dusted wax paper, extending it about 2 inches above can rims; secure with paper clips.

Beat dough to release air, then divide in half, placing each half in a lined can. Cover and let rise in a warm place until dough is within 1½ inches of top rim of can (about 1½ hours).

Bake on lowest rack of a 325° oven for 15 minutes; then reduce heat to 300° and bake for 45 minutes more. A slender wooden skewer inserted into breads should come out clean. Let breads stand in cans for 10 minutes, then turn out of cans and remove paper. Lay loaves horizontally on racks to cool; cradle them in folded towels to preserve shape. When cool, stand on end. Just before serving, glaze tops and decorate. Makes 2 loaves.

Glaze and decorations. Smoothly blend 1 cup unsifted **powdered sugar** with 1 tablespoon **lemon juice** and 1½ teaspoons **water**. Spread equally on tops of cooled loaves; let icing drizzle down sides of bread. Set small **rosebuds** (fresh or made of frosting) in glaze while still soft.

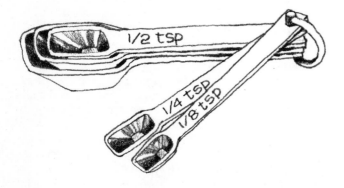

Hot Cross Buns

Though breads have been decorated with crosses since ancient times, the custom of serving hot cross buns at Easter probably began in 14th century England. According to legend, a kind-hearted monk baked them on Good Friday to feed the poor. As his gesture evolved into a seasonal tradition, many people believed the little breads contained sacred powers of protection. *(Photograph on facing page.)*

1 package active dry yeast
¼ cup warm water (about 110°)
1 cup warm milk (about 110°)
2 tablespoons butter or margarine
⅓ cup sugar
¾ teaspoon *each* salt and ground cinnamon
¼ teaspoon *each* ground cloves and nutmeg
2 eggs
¾ cup currants
¼ cup finely diced candied orange peel or citron
4⅓ to 4⅔ cups all-purpose flour, unsifted
1 egg yolk beaten with 1 tablespoon water
   Lemon frosting (recipe follows)

In a bowl, dissolve yeast in water. Stir in milk, butter, sugar, salt, cinnamon, cloves, and nutmeg. Beat in eggs. Add currants, orange peel, and enough of the flour (about 4 cups) to make a soft dough.

Turn dough out onto floured board; knead until smooth and satiny (10 to 20 minutes), adding flour as needed to prevent sticking. Turn dough over in a greased bowl; cover and let rise in a warm place until doubled (about 1½ hours).

Punch dough down and divide into 36 equal pieces; shape each into a smooth ball. Place balls about 2 inches apart on lightly greased baking sheets. Brush each gently with egg yolk mixture. Cover lightly and let rise in a warm place until doubled (about 35 minutes).

Bake in a 400° oven for about 10 minutes or until lightly browned. Cool on racks for about 5 minutes; then, with a spoon or the tip of a knife, drizzle frosting over top of each bun to make a small cross. Makes 3 dozen.

Lemon frosting. Combine 1 cup sifted **powdered sugar**, 2 teaspoons **lemon juice**, and 1 teaspoon **water**; beat until smooth.

Breads for Bakers in a Hurry

*Left to right: Herb Corn Sticks (page 87),
Sweet Breakfast Muffins (page 91), and
Banana-Apricot Nut Bread (page 84).*

Here are tasty little breads that you can whip up when you want to spend only an hour or so in the kitchen. Made without yeast, they require no rising time, and their mixing goes quickly.

Many are quietly nourishing, packed with such good things as fruits, nuts, seeds—even zucchini and carrots. Quick breads and muffins, tucked in lunch boxes or served as snacks, make a pleasant change of pace from routine fare. Try biscuits, scones, cornbread, and popovers as savory hot bread accompaniments to family meals.

Most quick breads keep well when tightly wrapped and stored in the refrigerator. Usually they become easier to slice and more flavorsome if you wait one day before serving.

Tangerine Oatmeal Loaf

Fresh tangerine peel and juice combine with rolled oats to flavor this moist fruit bread which is laden

with sweet chopped dates. Wrap loaf tightly to keep fresh at room temperature for about a week, or freeze for longer storage.

> 1 cup boiling water
> 1 package (about 8 oz.) pitted dates, chopped
> ¼ cup butter or margarine
> 1½ tablespoons grated tangerine or orange peel
> 1 cup fresh tangerine or orange juice
> 2 eggs, lightly beaten
> 2 cups *each* all-purpose flour, unsifted, and rolled oats, regular or quick-cooking
> ⅔ cup sugar
> 2 teaspoons *each* soda and baking powder
> 1 teaspoon salt
> 1 cup chopped walnuts

Pour boiling water over dates and butter. Stir until butter is melted; set aside. When mixture has cooled to room temperature, stir in tangerine peel, juice, and eggs. In a large bowl, stir together flour, oats, sugar, soda, baking powder, salt, and nuts until thoroughly blended. Add date mixture to dry ingredients and stir just until moistened.

Pour batter into a greased and flour-dusted 9 by 5-inch loaf pan (or into 2 pans each 3⅜ by 7⅜ inches).

Bake in a 350° oven for about 1 hour and 20 minutes (about 1 hour for the smaller pans), until bread begins to pull away from sides of pan and a wooden skewer inserted in center comes out clean. Let cool in pans for 10 minutes; then turn out onto a rack to cool completely. Makes 1 large or 2 small loaves.

Apple Brown Bread

Bits of fresh apple dot this wholesome molasses-flavored brown bread. A moist loaf, it slices more easily after maturing a day, and it's delicious served any time, plain, buttered, or with cream cheese.

- ½ cup (¼ lb.) butter or margarine
- ½ cup firmly packed brown sugar
- 1 egg
- ½ cup dark molasses
- 2 cups *each* all-purpose flour and graham flour, unsifted
- 2 teaspoons soda
- 1 teaspoon *each* baking powder and salt
- 2 cups *each* buttermilk and finely chopped, unpeeled, tart apple
- 1 cup chopped walnuts

Beat together butter and brown sugar until light and creamy. Beat in egg; then stir in molasses until blended. In another bowl, stir together all-purpose flour, graham flour, soda, baking powder, and salt until thoroughly blended. Add dry ingredients alternately with buttermilk to creamed mixture; after each addition mix just until blended. Stir in apple and nuts. Spoon batter into 2 greased and flour-dusted 4½ by 8½-inch pans (or into 3 pans, each 3⅜ by 7⅜ inches).

Bake in a 350° oven for about 1½ hours (about 1 hour and 15 minutes for smaller pans) or until bread begins to pull away from sides of pans and a wooden skewer inserted in center comes out clean. Let cool in pans for 10 minutes; then turn out onto a rack to cool completely. Makes 2 medium-size or 3 small loaves.

Wheat Germ Zucchini Bread

When your zucchini patch provides you with an abundant harvest, here is an appetizing and nutritious way to celebrate.

Use the coarsest surface of your grater to shred the zucchini. Also, be sure to blend the mixture gently when the zucchini is added to avoid crushing it and making the mixture wetter than desired. *(Photograph on page 78.)*

- 3 eggs
- 1 cup salad oil
- 1 cup *each* granulated sugar and firmly packed brown sugar
- 3 teaspoons maple flavoring
- 2 cups coarsely shredded unpeeled zucchini (about 4 medium-size)
- 2½ cups all-purpose flour, unsifted
- ½ cup toasted wheat germ
- 2 teaspoons *each* soda and salt
- ½ teaspoon baking powder
- 1 cup finely chopped walnuts
- ⅓ cup sesame seed

Beat eggs until frothy; add oil, sugars, and maple flavoring, and continue beating until mixture is thick and foamy. Stir in shredded zucchini. In a separate bowl, stir together flour, wheat germ, soda, salt, baking powder, and walnuts until thoroughly blended; stir gently into zucchini mixture just until blended. Spoon the batter equally into 2 greased and flour-dusted 9 by 5-inch loaf pans. Sprinkle sesame seed evenly over top of each.

Bake in a 350° oven for 1 hour or until bread begins to pull away from sides of pans and a wooden skewer inserted in center comes out clean. Let cool in pans for 10 minutes; then turn out onto a rack to cool completely. Makes 2 loaves.

Spicy Pineapple-Zucchini Bread

Versatile zucchini combines happily with pineapple in this moist, tender bread that is flecked with green.

- 3 eggs
- 1 cup salad oil
- 2 cups sugar
- 2 teaspoons vanilla
- 2 cups coarsely shredded, unpeeled zucchini
- 1 can (8¼ oz.) well-drained crushed pineapple
- 3 cups all-purpose flour, unsifted
- 2 teaspoons soda
- 1 teaspoon salt
- ½ teaspoon baking powder
- 1½ teaspoons ground cinnamon
- ¾ teaspoon ground nutmeg
- 1 cup *each* finely chopped walnuts and currants

In a large bowl, beat eggs until frothy; add oil, sugar, and vanilla; continue beating until mixture is thick and foamy. Stir in zucchini and pineapple. In a separate bowl, stir together flour, soda, salt, baking powder, cinnamon, nutmeg, walnuts, and currants until thoroughly blended. Stir gently into zucchini mixture just until blended. Spoon batter equally into 2 greased and flour-dusted 9 by 5-inch loaf pans.

(Continued on page 79)

Spicy fragrances fill the kitchen when you bake (clockwise from lower left) Whole Wheat Dinner Muffins (page 93), Currant Soda Bread (page 86), Wheat Germ Zucchini Bread (page 77), and Apricot Nut Loaves (page 80).

... *Spicy Pineapple-Zucchini Bread (cont'd.)*

Bake in a 350° oven for 1 hour or until breads begin to pull away from sides of pans and a wooden skewer inserted in centers comes out clean. Let cool in pans for 10 minutes; then turn out onto racks to cool completely. Makes 2 loaves.

Pumpkin-Pecan Tea Loaf

Fragrances of pumpkin and blended spices characterize this bread that is made in part from whole wheat flour. For a special breakfast treat, cut into thick slices and toast lightly.

- ⅔ **cup shortening**
- 2⅔ **cups sugar**
- 4 **eggs**
- 1 **can (1 lb.) pumpkin**
- ⅔ **cup water**
- 2½ **cups all-purpose flour, unsifted**
- 1 **cup whole wheat flour, unsifted**
- 2 **teaspoons soda**
- 1½ **teaspoons salt**
- ½ **teaspoon baking powder**
- ½ **teaspoon ground cardamom (optional)**
- 1 **teaspoon** *each* **ground cloves and ground cinnamon**
- 1 **cup** *each* **raisins and chopped pecans**

Beat together shortening and sugar until well blended. Beat in eggs. Add pumpkin and water; stir until blended. In another bowl, stir together all-purpose flour, whole wheat flour, soda, salt, baking powder, cardamom, cloves, and cinnamon until thoroughly blended. Gradually add these dry ingredients to pumpkin mixture and stir until well blended. Stir in raisins and chopped pecans. Pour batter into 2 greased and flour-dusted 9 by 5-inch pans (or in 3 pans each 3⅜ by 7⅜ inches).

Bake in a 350° oven for about 1 hour and 15 minutes (about 1 hour for smaller pans), until bread begins to pull away from sides of pans and a wooden skewer inserted in center comes out clean. Let cool in pans for 10 minutes; then turn out onto a rack to cool completely. Makes 2 medium-size or 3 small loaves.

Fresh Apple Fruit Loaf

Packed with fruits and nuts and flavored with sherry, this moist, crunchy bread may remind you of fruitcake.

- 1 **cup firmly packed brown sugar**
- ½ **cup salad oil**
- 2 **tablespoons dry sherry**
- 1 **teaspoon vanilla**
- 1 **cup** *each* **raisins, coarsely chopped mixed candied fruit, chopped nuts, and pitted dates cut in small pieces**
- 1½ **cups coarsely shredded, peeled raw apples**
- 2 **teaspoons soda**
- 2 **cups all-purpose flour, unsifted**
- ½ **teaspoon salt**
- ¼ **teaspoon** *each* **ground cinnamon and ground nutmeg**

In a large bowl, mix together brown sugar, oil, sherry, and vanilla. Stir in raisins, candied fruit, nuts, and dates. Mix apples with soda until thoroughly combined; stir into fruit-nut mixture. In a separate bowl, stir together flour, salt, cinnamon, and nutmeg until well blended; then add to fruit mixture, stirring to blend thoroughly. Turn into a greased and flour-dusted 9 by 5-inch loaf pan.

Bake in a 350° oven for 1 hour and 25 minutes, until bread begins to pull away from sides of pan and a wooden skewer inserted in center comes out clean. Let cool in pan for about 3 minutes; then turn out onto a rack to cool completely. Wrap and refrigerate for 1 day before slicing. Makes 1 loaf.

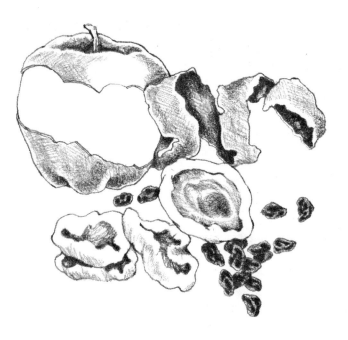

Poppy Seed Loaf

Crunchy poppy seeds give an exciting burst of flavor to this mellow, moist tea bread. Offered with a tangy apricot spread, it's a good choice to serve with mid-morning coffee or with a fruit salad for lunch.

 ¼ cup butter or margarine
 1 cup sugar
 2 eggs
 1 teaspoon grated orange peel
 2 cups all-purpose flour, unsifted
 2½ teaspoons baking powder
 ½ teaspoon salt
 ¼ teaspoon ground nutmeg
 1 cup milk
 ⅓ cup poppy seed
 ½ cup chopped nuts
 ½ cup golden raisins (optional)
   Tangy apricot spread (recipe follows)

Beat together butter and sugar until smoothly blended; add eggs, one at a time, beating well after each addition. Mix in orange peel. In a separate bowl, stir together flour, baking powder, salt, and nutmeg until thoroughly blended. Add flour mixture alternately with milk to creamed mixture until well blended, then stir in poppy seed, nuts, and raisins, if used. Turn batter into a well-greased and flour-dusted 9 by 5-inch loaf pan.

Bake in a 350° oven for 1 hour and 10 minutes or until bread begins to pull away from sides of pan and a wooden skewer inserted in center comes out clean. Let cool in pan for 10 minutes, then turn out onto a rack to cool completely. Makes 1 loaf.

Tangy apricot spread. Beat together ½ cup soft **butter** or margarine, ¼ cup **apricot jam**, 1 teaspoon grated **lemon peel**, and 1 tablespoon **lemon juice**.

Apricot Nut Loaf

Tangy apricots and plump raisins mingle with walnuts in this moist and richly flavored bread. *(Photograph on page 78.)*

 ¾ cup dried apricots
   Lukewarm water
 1 orange (juice and rind)
 ½ cup raisins
   Boiling water
 ⅔ cup sugar
 2 tablespoons butter or margarine, melted
 1 egg
 2 cups all-purpose flour, unsifted
 2 teaspoons baking powder
 1 teaspoon *each* salt and soda
 ½ cup chopped walnuts
 1 teaspoon vanilla

Cover apricots with lukewarm water and let stand for 30 minutes; drain. Use a vegetable peeler to remove thin outer peel from half the orange; then ream all juice from both halves. Force apricots, raisins, and the thin orange peel through medium blade of a food grinder (or finely chop with a knife). Add enough boiling water to orange juice to make 1 cup and pour into bowl with ground fruit. Mix in sugar and butter; beat in egg. In a separate bowl, stir together flour, baking powder, salt, and soda until thoroughly blended. Stir dry ingredients into apricot mixture until blended. Add nuts and vanilla. Spoon into a well-greased 9 by 5-inch loaf pan.

Bake in a 350° oven for 50 minutes or until bread begins to pull away from sides of pan and a wooden skewer inserted in center comes out clean. Let cool in pan for 10 minutes; then turn out onto a rack to cool completely. Makes 1 loaf.

Where did pumpernickel get its curious name? One story links it to Napoleon's reaction when he tasted the rather coarse, inelegant bread. Feeding it to his horse, he cried: "Bon pour Nicol!" (or, good for Nicol, the horse).

Honey Peanut Loaf

Tucked in lunch boxes or served for snacks, this honey-sweetened loaf will win applause from peanut butter fans.

 ½ cup *each* butter or margarine, at room temperature, and chunk-style peanut butter
 ¼ cup firmly packed brown sugar
 2 eggs
 ½ cup honey
 1 teaspoon vanilla
 ½ cup buttermilk
 2 cups all-purpose flour, unsifted
 1 teaspoon *each* baking powder and soda
 ⅛ teaspoon salt

In a large bowl beat together butter, peanut butter, and brown sugar until well blended. Add eggs one at a time and beat until fluffy. Stir in honey, vanilla, and buttermilk. In a separate bowl, stir together flour, baking powder, soda, and salt until thoroughly blended. Mix into creamed mixture. Spoon batter into a greased 9 by 5-inch loaf pan.

Bake in a 325° oven for 55 minutes or until bread begins to pull away from sides of pan and a wooden skewer inserted in center comes out clean. Cool in pan for 10 minutes; then turn out onto a rack to cool completely. Makes 1 loaf.

Raisin-Nut Honey Bread

A touch of honey sweetens and perfumes this fragrant nut bread—a good choice to accompany a luncheon fruit salad or afternoon tea.

- ½ cup *each* butter or margarine, at room temperature, and firmly packed brown sugar
- 2 eggs
- ½ cup *each* honey and buttermilk
- 2 cups all-purpose flour, unsifted
- 1 teaspoon soda
- ½ teaspoon *each* ground ginger and ground cloves
- 2 teaspoons ground cinnamon
- ¼ teaspoon salt
- ½ cup *each* raisins and chopped walnuts

In a large bowl beat together butter and sugar until smoothly blended. Add eggs, one at a time, and beat until fluffy. Blend in honey and buttermilk. In a separate bowl, stir together flour, soda, ginger, cloves, cinnamon, and salt until thoroughly blended; mix into creamed mixture. Stir in raisins and nuts. Spoon batter into a greased 9 by 5-inch loaf pan.

Bake in a 325° oven for 1 hour or until bread begins to pull away from sides of pan and a wooden skewer inserted in center comes out clean. Cool in pan for 10 minutes; then turn out onto a rack to cool completely. Makes 1 loaf.

Date Nut Loaf

Laden with dates, this dark, rich-tasting bread is delicious when spread with soft cheese such as cream cheese or breakfast cheese.

- 1¼ cups all-purpose flour, unsifted
- 1 teaspoon *each* baking powder and soda
- ½ cup sugar
- ¼ teaspoon salt
- ½ teaspoon ground cinnamon
- 1 package (8 oz.) pitted dates, chopped
- ½ cup *each* golden raisins and chopped walnuts
- 2 tablespoons butter or margarine
- ½ teaspoon vanilla
- 1 cup hot water
- 1 egg

In a large bowl stir together flour, baking powder, soda, sugar, salt, cinnamon, dates, raisins, and walnuts until thoroughly blended. In a separate bowl, stir together butter, vanilla, and hot water until butter is melted; then stir in egg. Pour butter mixture into dry ingredients and stir just until well blended. Pour batter into a greased 4½ by 8½-inch loaf pan.

Bake in a 325° oven for 1 hour and 25 minutes or until bread begins to pull away from sides of pan and a wooden skewer inserted in center comes out clean. (Or bake 1 hour in a 9 by 5-inch pan, or 45 minutes in 2 pans, each 3⅜ by 7⅜ inches.) Let cool in pan for 10 minutes; then turn out onto a rack to cool completely. Makes 1 large or 2 small loaves.

Honey Raisin Bread

Plump, golden raisins permeate this honey-flavored bread. A small addition of bran contributes heartiness to its texture.

- 2½ cups all-purpose flour, unsifted
- 3 teaspoons baking powder
- ½ teaspoon soda
- 1 teaspoon salt
- ½ cup whole bran cereal
- ⅓ cup firmly packed light brown sugar
- 1 cup golden raisins
- ½ cup chopped walnuts or pecans
- 1 cup milk
- 2 eggs
- ⅓ cup honey
- 2 tablespoons butter or margarine, melted

In a large bowl stir together flour, baking powder, soda, salt, cereal, sugar, raisins, and nuts until thoroughly blended. In a separate bowl, combine milk,

(Continued on page 83)

Three Scandinavian Flatbreads

Flatbreads—often crisp and crackly but sometimes soft and pliable—appear in many different cuisines of the world. Here are three tasty versions from Scandinavia.

Rieska

This wheatless bread, a tradition in northern Finland and Lapland, is best served hot from the oven, spread with butter. Look for the barley flour at a health food store.

> 2 cups barley flour or rye flour, unsifted, or 1 cup of *each* flour
> ¾ teaspoon salt
> 2 teaspoons *each* sugar and baking powder
> 1 cup evaporated milk or light cream
> 2 tablespoons butter, melted

In a large bowl, stir together flour, salt, sugar, and baking powder until well blended. Stir in milk and melted butter until a smooth dough forms. Turn dough out onto a well-buttered baking sheet and, with flour-dusted hands, pat dough out to make a circle about 14 inches in diameter and ½ inch thick. Prick all over with a fork.

Bake in a 450° oven for 10 minutes or until lightly browned. Serve immediately. Makes 8 to 10 rounds.

Norwegian Potato Lefse

Soft, thin, chewy, and slightly sour, this Norwegian bread bakes on a griddle or heavy frying pan. Try it wrapped around sausages or fingers of cheese or simply spread with butter and sprinkled with sugar.

> About 2½ pounds baking potatoes
> Boiling water
> 2 tablespoons butter or margarine
> ¼ cup milk
> 1 teaspoon salt
> 3 to 3½ cups all-purpose flour, unsifted
> Salad oil

Peel potatoes and cut into quarters; cover with boiling water and cook until fork tender (about 30 minutes).

Drain and mash until very smooth. Measure potatoes; you should have 4 cups. Stir in butter, milk, and salt, mixing well. Let cool to room temperature.

Gradually mix in enough of the flour (about 2 cups) to make a nonsticky dough. On a floured board, knead gently to shape into a smooth log. Divide into 24 equal pieces; do not cover.

If possible, cover rolling pin with stockinet. Shape each piece of dough into a smooth ball. On a pastry cloth or floured board, roll each ball into a thin 8 to 10-inch round. Turn rounds and keep coated with flour (using as little as possible) to prevent sticking.

Preheat an electric griddle or frying pan to 375° or use a griddle or frying pan over medium heat. Lightly grease with oil.

Shake excess flour off each round and place in pan. It will start to bubble; bake until bubbles are lightly browned (about 1½ minutes). With a spatula, turn and bake other side. Serve warm. Or let cool on racks; wrap airtight. Refrigerate for up to 4 days, or freeze. To reheat (thaw first, if frozen), stack and wrap in foil; place in a 325° oven for 10 to 15 minutes. Makes 24.

Swedish Flatbread

These thin, fragile, crisp rounds look like oversize crackers. You can store them in an airtight container for 2 to 3 weeks.

> 2¾ cups all-purpose flour, unsifted
> ¼ cup sugar
> ½ teaspoon *each* soda and salt
> ½ cup (¼ lb.) butter or margarine
> 1 cup buttermilk

In a large bowl, stir together flour, sugar, soda, and salt until well blended. With a pastry cutter or 2 knives, cut in butter until mixture resembles fine crumbs. Using a fork, stir in buttermilk until mixture holds together.

Shape into a ball; break off pieces about 1 inch in diameter. Roll each on a floured board to make a round 4 to 5 inches in diameter, turning occasionally to prevent sticking. Place rounds slightly apart on ungreased baking sheets.

Bake in a 400° oven for 5 minutes or until lightly browned; check frequently. Cool on racks. Makes about 6 dozen.

eggs, honey, and butter; stir into dry ingredients just until well blended. Pour batter into a greased 4½ by 8½-inch loaf pan.

Bake in a 350° oven for 1 hour and 15 minutes or until bread begins to pull away from sides of pan and a wooden skewer inserted in center comes out clean. (Bake 1 hour in a 9 by 5-inch pan, or 45 minutes in 2 pans, each 3⅜ by 7⅜ inches.) Let cool in pan for 10 minutes; then turn out onto a rack to cool completely. Makes 1 large or 2 small loaves.

French Honey Bread

This firm-textured tea bread from France is called *pain d'épice*. Typically, it is sliced thin and spread with soft butter or cream cheese.

2⅔ cups all-purpose flour, unsifted
  1 teaspoon *each* ground cinnamon and soda
  ½ teaspoon *each* ground nutmeg and ground cloves
  ¼ teaspoon salt
  ¼ cup firmly packed brown sugar
  ¾ cup honey
  1 small can (about 6 oz.) evaporated milk
  ⅓ cup milk

Stir together flour, cinnamon, soda, nutmeg, cloves, and salt until thoroughly blended. Mix in brown sugar. In another bowl, beat together honey, evaporated milk, and milk; add to dry ingredients and stir just until blended. Pour into a greased and flour-dusted 9 by 5-inch loaf pan.

Bake in a 325° oven for 1 hour and 10 minutes, until bread begins to pull away from sides of pan and a wooden skewer inserted in the center comes out clean. Let cool in pan for 5 minutes, then turn out onto a rack to cool completely.

Wrap and store for 1 day before serving. Makes 1 loaf.

Carrot Bread

This spicy loaf has an intriguing flavor, fine texture, and a crisp crust. To make round loaves, you can bake this bread in 1-pound vegetable or fruit cans.

  4 eggs
  2 cups sugar
1¼ cups salad oil
  3 cups all-purpose flour, unsifted
  2 teaspoons baking powder
1½ teaspoons soda
  ¼ teaspoon salt
  2 teaspoons ground cinnamon
  2 cups finely shredded raw carrots

Beat eggs; then gradually add sugar, beating until thick. Gradually add oil and continue beating until thoroughly blended. In a separate bowl, stir together flour, baking powder, soda, salt, and cinnamon until thoroughly blended. Mix dry ingredients into egg mixture until smooth and well blended. Stir in the carrots. Spoon into 2 well-greased 9 by 5-inch loaf pans (or 4 well-greased 1-pound cans, filling them no more than ⅔ full).

Bake in a 350° oven for 1 hour (45 minutes for 1-pound cans) or until a wooden skewer inserted in center comes out clean. Makes 2 medium-size or 4 small loaves.

Banana Coconut Bread

Chewy with shreds of coconut, this banana loaf makes a wholesome after-school snack. Also try it lightly toasted for breakfast. You can buy the unsweetened coconut where health foods are sold.

  2 cups all-purpose flour, unsifted
  1 teaspoon soda
  ¾ teaspoon salt
  ½ cup soft butter or margarine
  1 cup firmly packed brown sugar
  2 eggs
  1 teaspoon vinegar mixed with 1 tablespoon milk
  1 teaspoon vanilla
1½ cups mashed ripe banana (about 3 to 4)
  1 cup unsweetened shredded coconut

Stir together flour, soda, and salt until thoroughly blended. In a large bowl, beat butter and sugar together until creamy. Add eggs, one at a time, beating well after each addition; beat in vinegar mixture, vanilla, and bananas. Gradually stir in flour mixture just until blended; stir in coconut. Pour batter into a greased and flour-dusted 9 by 5-inch loaf pan.

Bake in a 350° oven for 1 hour and 15 minutes, until bread begins to pull away from sides of pan and a wooden skewer inserted in center comes out clean. Let cool in pan 10 minutes; then turn out on a rack to cool completely. Wrap and store for 1 day before slicing. Makes 1 loaf.

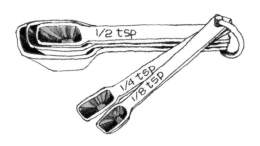

Whole Wheat Banana Bread

Whole wheat flour lends full-bodied flavor to this moist banana bread, which has a light, cakelike texture.

- ½ cup (¼ lb.) butter or margarine
- 1 cup sugar
- 2 eggs, lightly beaten
- 1 cup *each* mashed ripe banana (about 3) and all-purpose flour, unsifted
- ½ teaspoon salt
- 1 teaspoon soda
- 1 cup whole wheat flour, unsifted
- ⅓ cup hot water
- ½ cup chopped walnuts

Melt butter and blend in sugar. Mix in beaten eggs and mashed banana, blending until smooth. In a bowl, stir together all-purpose flour, salt, soda, and whole wheat flour until thoroughly blended. Add dry ingredients alternately with hot water. Stir in chopped nuts. Spoon batter into a greased 9 by 5-inch loaf pan.

Bake in a 325° oven for about 1 hour and 10 minutes, until bread begins to pull away from sides of pan and a wooden skewer inserted in center comes out clean. Let cool in pan for 10 minutes; then turn out onto a rack to cool completely. Makes 1 loaf.

Banana-Apricot Nut Bread

Tangy apricots, liberally laced through this fruit-and-nut bread, blend with the more delicate flavor of ripe banana to make a rich-tasting, moist, and tender treat.

- 2 cups all-purpose flour, unsifted
- 1 teaspoon baking powder
- ½ teaspoon *each* soda and salt
- 1 cup sugar
- ½ cup *each* chopped dried apricots and walnuts
- ¾ cup mashed ripe banana
- ½ cup milk
- 1 egg
- ¼ cup melted butter or margarine

In a bowl, stir together the flour, baking powder, soda, salt, sugar, apricots, and nuts until thoroughly blended. In a separate bowl, combine banana, milk, egg, and butter; stir into the dry ingredients just until well blended. Pour batter into a greased 4½ by 8½-inch loaf pan.

Bake in a 350° oven for 1 hour and 15 minutes, until bread begins to pull away from sides of pan and a wooden skewer inserted in center comes out clean. (Or bake 1 hour in a 9 by 5-inch pan, or 45 minutes in 2 pans, each 3⅜ by 7⅜ inches.) Let cool in pan for 10 minutes; then turn out onto a rack to cool completely. Makes 1 large or 2 small loaves.

Whole Wheat Prune Bread

Nourishing and delicious, this versatile bread will please the family for breakfast, lunch, snacks—even for dessert.

- 1½ cups whole wheat flour, unsifted
- ½ cup all-purpose flour, unsifted
- 1 teaspoon *each* salt and soda
- ½ teaspoon *each* baking powder and ground cinnamon
- ¼ cup butter or margarine
- ¾ cup firmly packed brown sugar
- 1 egg
- 1 cup buttermilk
- 1 package (12 oz.) moist-pack pitted prunes, chopped
- ⅔ cup chopped walnuts

Stir together whole wheat and all-purpose flours, salt, soda, baking powder, and cinnamon until thoroughly blended; set aside. In a separate bowl, beat together butter and brown sugar until creamy, then beat in egg. Alternately add flour mixture and buttermilk to creamed mixture. With last addition of flour mixture, add prunes and nuts, stirring until blended. Spoon into a well-greased 9 by 5-inch loaf pan.

Bake in a 350° oven for about 1 hour and 10 minutes or until bread begins to pull away from sides of pan and a wooden skewer inserted in center comes out clean. Let cool in pan for 10 minutes; then turn out onto a rack to cool completely. Wrap and store in refrigerator for 1 day before slicing. Makes 1 loaf.

Orange Prune Loaf

This moist prune-and-nut bread is flavored with orange peel and moistened with cottage cheese.

     2 cups all-purpose flour, unsifted
  1½ teaspoons baking powder
     ½ teaspoon *each* soda and salt
     ½ cup (¼ lb.) butter or margarine
     ⅔ cup firmly packed brown sugar
     4 teaspoons grated orange peel
     1 egg
     1 cup (8 oz.) small curd cottage cheese
     1 cup moist-pack pitted prunes, chopped
     ½ cup chopped walnuts
     ¼ cup milk

Stir together flour, baking powder, soda, and salt until thoroughly blended; set aside. In a separate bowl, beat butter and brown sugar together until creamy. Add orange peel and egg and beat until fluffy. Mix in cottage cheese and half the flour mixture. Combine remaining flour mixture with prunes and nuts; then stir in milk until well blended. Stir into first flour mixture until well blended. Spoon batter into a well greased 9 by 5-inch loaf pan.

Bake in a 350° oven for about 1 hour and 10 minutes or until loaf begins to pull away from sides of pan and a wooden skewer inserted in center comes out clean. Let cool in pan for 10 minutes; then turn out onto a rack to cool completely. Wrap and store overnight at room temperature before slicing. Makes 1 loaf.

Rhubarb Tea Bread

Dark, rich, and spicy, this tea bread is made with bits of fresh rhubarb, which lend it a moist texture and a hint of tartness.

     3 eggs
     1 cup salad oil
     2 cups firmly packed brown sugar
     2 teaspoons vanilla
  2½ cups finely diced fresh rhubarb
     ½ cup chopped walnuts
     3 cups all-purpose flour (or 1½ cups *each*
          all-purpose and whole wheat flour),
          unsifted
     2 teaspoons soda
     1 teaspoon salt
     ½ teaspoon *each* baking powder, ground
          nutmeg, and ground allspice
     2 teaspoons ground cinnamon

In a large bowl, beat together eggs, oil, sugar, and vanilla until thick and foamy. Stir in rhubarb and nuts. In a separate bowl, combine flour(s) with soda, salt, baking powder, nutmeg, allspice, and cinnamon;

stir until thoroughly blended. Add dry ingredients to rhubarb mixture, stirring gently just until blended. Spoon batter into two greased 9 by 5-inch loaf pans.

Bake in a 350° oven for 1 hour or until bread begins to pull away from sides of pans and a wooden skewer inserted in center comes out clean. Let cool in pans for 10 minutes; then turn out onto a rack to cool completely. Makes 2 loaves.

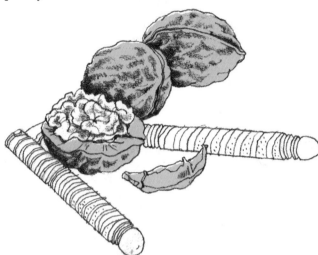

Cottage Cheese Fruit Bread

Cottage cheese adds moistness to this bread, which is laced with apricots and dates and delicately flavored with orange and lemon peel.

     ½ cup butter or margarine
     ¾ cup firmly packed brown sugar
     ½ teaspoon *each* grated orange and lemon
          peel
     2 eggs
  1½ cups creamed small curd cottage cheese
  2½ cups all-purpose flour, unsifted
     3 teaspoons baking powder
     1 teaspoon *each* soda and salt
     1 cup chopped dried apricots
     1 cup chopped pitted dates

Beat together butter, sugar, orange and lemon peel until creamy. Mix in eggs and cottage cheese until well blended. In a separate bowl, stir together flour, baking powder, soda, and salt until thoroughly blended. Add apricots and dates to flour mixture, mixing until well coated.

Add flour mixture to butter mixture, stirring until well blended (batter will be very stiff). Spread batter, smoothing top with a spatula, into 2 greased and flour-dusted 8½ by 4½-inch loaf pans.

Bake in a 350° oven for 40 to 45 minutes or until bread begins to pull away from sides of pan and a wooden skewer inserted in center comes out clean. Let cool in pan for about 10 minutes; then turn out onto a rack to cool completely. Makes 2 loaves.

Graham Yogurt Bread

This wholesome, even-textured bread bakes in three 1-pound cans—the kind used for canned fruits and vegetables. Tightly wrapped and stored in the refrigerator, these loaves stay fresh for about 5 days.

    2   cups graham flour, unsifted
    ½   cup all-purpose flour, unsifted
    2   teaspoons soda
    1   teaspoon salt
    2   cups unflavored yogurt
    ½   cup molasses
    1   cup raisins
    ½   cup chopped walnuts

Remove one end from each of three 1-pound cans; rinse cans, dry, and grease well. In a large bowl, stir together graham flour, all-purpose flour, soda, and salt until thoroughly blended. Stir in yogurt, molasses, raisins, and walnuts; mix well. Divide batter evenly into cans.

Bake in a 350° oven for about 1 hour or until a wooden skewer inserted in center comes out clean. Cool in cans for about 10 minutes; then turn out and stand loaves upright on a rack to cool completely. Makes 3 small loaves.

Brown Bread

Try thick slices of this dark, rich-tasting bread with baked beans and your favorite sausages for supper. Tightly wrapped and kept in the refrigerator, it stays fresh for several days.

    3   tablespoons butter or margarine
    ¾   cup firmly packed brown sugar
    2   cups buttermilk
    3   tablespoons light molasses
    2   cups whole wheat or graham flour,
          unsifted
    1   cup all-purpose flour, unsifted
    ½   cup wheat germ
    2   teaspoons soda
    1   teaspoon salt
    1   cup *each* raisins and chopped walnuts

In a large bowl beat butter and sugar together until creamy. Then mix in buttermilk and molasses. In a separate bowl, stir together the whole wheat flour, all-purpose flour, wheat germ, soda, and salt until thoroughly blended. Add to the buttermilk mixture and beat until well combined. Stir in raisins and chopped nuts. Spoon batter into a well-greased 9 by 5-inch loaf pan.

Bake in a 350° oven for 1 hour and 20 minutes or until bread begins to pull away from sides of pan and

a wooden skewer inserted in center comes out clean. Let cool in pan 10 minutes; then turn out onto a rack to cool completely. Makes 1 loaf.

Irish Soda Bread

In Dublin, rounds of soda bread accompany every meal, from breakfast to high tea. Each warm, thick slice makes a delectable platter for butter and honey or marmalade.

Fruited and whole wheat variations follow our basic recipe.

    4   to 4¼ cups all-purpose flour, unsifted
    1   teaspoon salt
    3   teaspoons baking powder
    1   teaspoon soda
    ¼   cup sugar (optional)
    ⅛   teaspoon ground cardamom or coriander
          (optional)
    ¼   cup butter or margarine
    1   egg
    1¾ cups buttermilk

In a large bowl stir together 4 cups of the flour, salt, baking powder, soda, and sugar and cardamom (if used) until thoroughly blended. Cut in butter with a pastry blender or two knives until crumbly. In a separate bowl, beat egg slightly and mix with buttermilk; stir into dry ingredients until blended. Turn out on a floured board and knead until smooth (2 to 3 minutes).

Divide dough in half and shape each half into a smooth, round loaf; place each loaf in a greased 8-inch cake or pie pan. Press down until dough fills pans. With a razor blade or sharp, floured knife, cut crosses in tops of loaves, about ½ inch deep.

Bake in a 375° oven for 35 to 40 minutes or until nicely browned. Makes 2 loaves.

Currant Soda Bread

Follow recipe for Irish Soda Bread (above), including sugar but omitting cardamom and coriander. After cutting in butter, add 2 cups **currants or raisins** and 1¼ teaspoons **caraway seed** (optional). Add egg and buttermilk and proceed as directed in recipe.

Whole Wheat Soda Bread

Follow recipe for Irish Soda Bread (above), but substitute 2 cups **whole wheat flour** for 2 cups of the all-purpose flour. After cutting in butter, add 1 to 2 cups **raisins** or chopped **dates**, if you wish. (*Photograph on page 78.*)

Panettone

Baked in a paper bag, this version of a traditional Milanese bread is moderately sweet and has a cakelike texture.

    1   egg
    2   egg yolks
  ¾   cup sugar
  ½   cup (¼ lb.) butter or margarine, melted
          and cooled
    1   teaspoon grated lemon peel
    1   teaspoon *each* anise seed and anise extract
  ¼   cup *each* pine nuts, raisins, and coarsely
          chopped, mixed candied fruit
  2⅔ cups all-purpose flour (sift before
          measuring)
    2   teaspoons baking powder
  ½   teaspoon salt
    1   cup milk

In a large bowl, beat egg, egg yolks, and sugar together until thick and pale yellow. Beat in butter; then add lemon peel, anise seed, anise extract, nuts, raisins and candied fruit. Stir together flour, baking powder, and salt. Blend half the dry ingredients into egg mixture. Stir in half the milk, add remaining dry ingredients, and mix well. Add remaining milk and blend thoroughly.

Fold down top of a paper bag (one that measures 3½ by 6 inches on the bottom) to form a cuff about 2¾ inches deep. Butter inside of bag generously, set on a baking sheet, and pour in batter.

Bake in a 325° oven for about 1 hour and 45 minutes or until well browned and a wooden skewer inserted in the center comes out clean. To serve hot, tear off paper bag and cut bread into wedges. To serve cold, wrap bread (still in bag) in a cloth, then in foil, and let cool completely to mellow the flavors. Makes 1 loaf.

Sesame Wheat Germ Cornbread

Toasted sesame seeds lend a hearty, nutlike flavor and crunchiness to this cornbread.

  1½   cups all-purpose flour, unsifted
  ½   cup sugar
  1½   teaspoons salt
  1¼   teaspoons soda
    2   cups cornmeal
    1   cup wheat germ
  ½   cup sesame seeds, toasted
    2   cups buttermilk
  ¾   cup salad oil or melted butter or
          margarine
    2   eggs, lightly beaten

In a large bowl, stir together flour, sugar, salt, and soda until thoroughly blended. Mix in cornmeal, wheat germ, and sesame seeds. In a separate bowl, mix together buttermilk, salad oil or melted butter, and eggs. Stir liquid mixture into dry ingredients just until blended. Pour into a greased 9 by 5-inch loaf pan.

Bake in a 375° oven for about 55 minutes or until a wooden skewer inserted in center comes out clean. Let cool in pan for 5 minutes; then turn out onto a rack to cool completely. Makes 1 large loaf.

We owe our traditional American cornbread to Indians who introduced many delicacies made from corn to early settlers. The Algonquins' version, called "appone," gradually became known as "corn pone."

Herb Corn Sticks

These light-textured corn sticks have a subtle herb flavor. Serve them as savory companions to a salad or soup or as a quick-to-make dinner bread.

  1⅔ cups all-purpose flour, unsifted
    3   teaspoons baking powder
  ¾   teaspoon salt
    2   tablespoons sugar
  ¾   cup yellow cornmeal
  ½   teaspoon crumbled marjoram leaves
    1   teaspoon crumbled thyme leaves
    1   egg
  1½   cups milk
  ¼   cup butter or margarine, melted

In a large bowl, stir together flour, baking powder, salt, and sugar until thoroughly blended. Mix in cornmeal, marjoram, and thyme. In a separate bowl, beat egg, then stir in milk and melted butter; add all at once to dry ingredients and stir just until mixture is moistened. Spoon into well-greased corn stick pans, filling about ¾ full.

Bake in a 425° oven for 15 to 18 minutes or until golden brown. Makes about 21 corn sticks.

Mexican Cornbread

Borrowing flavors from Mexico, this savory cornbread combines Cheddar cheese with green chiles. Sour cream adds rich moistness while the creamed corn contributes texture. To control the heat-taste level of the cornbread's seasonings, sample a small piece of each chile, since their potency varies.

(Continued on next page)

2 eggs
¼ cup salad oil
1 to 4 canned California green chiles
1 small can (about 9 oz.) creamed-style corn
½ cup sour cream
1 cup yellow cornmeal
½ teaspoon salt
2 teaspoons baking powder
2 cups (about 8 oz.) shredded sharp
   Cheddar cheese

In a large bowl, beat eggs and oil until well blended. Rinse seeds out of chiles, finely chop chiles, and add to egg mixture. Then add corn, sour cream, cornmeal, salt, baking powder, and 1½ cups of the cheese; stir until thoroughly blended. Pour into a greased 8 or 9-inch round or square pan. Sprinkle remaining ½ cup cheese evenly over the top.

Bake in a 350° oven for 1 hour or until a wooden skewer inserted in center comes out clean and crust is lightly browned. Makes 6 to 8 servings.

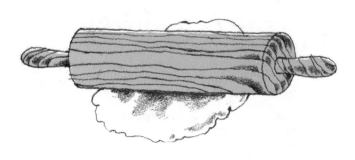

Blue Cheese Crisps

These blue cheese triangles can be made several hours ahead and baked just before serving. You can also bake them, freeze them, and have them ready to heat when they are needed. Serve as a salad accompaniment or as the bread for supper.

1 package (4 oz.) blue cheese
½ cup soft butter or margarine
1 egg, separated
2 tablespoons milk or cream
1 cup all-purpose flour, unsifted
   Paprika

Beat together cheese, butter, egg yolk, and milk or cream until smooth. Stir flour into creamed mixture. Turn out on a lightly floured board and knead just until blended, about 5 turns. Divide dough in half, form each half into a ball, wrap in wax paper, and chill.

When dough is firm, roll out one ball at a time on a lightly floured board to a circle about 12 inches in diameter and ⅛ inch thick. Cut into 12 wedges and place on a lightly greased baking sheet. Brush each triangle with slightly beaten egg white and sprinkle lightly with paprika. Repeat for second ball of dough.

Bake in a 400° oven about 10 minutes or until crisp and lightly browned. Makes 2 dozen.

Sesame Swirls

If your family favors biscuits, you might want to serve these toasted sesame seed-filled biscuit rolls with your next barbecue.

½ cup sesame seed
2 tablespoons butter or margarine
2½ cups all-purpose flour, unsifted
2½ teaspoons baking powder
1 teaspoon salt
½ cup butter or margarine
1 cup sour cream
½ cup milk
1 egg, slightly beaten

Sauté sesame seed with the 2 tablespoons butter until seed and butter are lightly browned; set aside to cool. Stir together flour, baking powder and salt until thoroughly blended. Cut in the ½ cup butter with a pastry blender or 2 knives. In a separate bowl, stir together sour cream and milk and add to flour mixture, blending gently. Turn out on a lightly floured board and knead dough gently about 5 times.

Roll dough to a rectangle about 15 inches long, 12 inches wide, and ¼ inch thick. Brush with half of beaten egg, then spread with sesame seed mixture. Starting with long side, roll up jelly-roll fashion; pinch edge to seal. Cut roll with a floured knife into 1-inch slices and place slices, cut side up, on a lightly greased baking sheet. Brush with remaining egg.

Bake in a 425° oven for about 15 minutes or until lightly browned. Makes 16 biscuits.

French Cheese Puffs

The French serve this savory Swiss cheese bread, called *gougère*, for lunch, with a mixed green salad and red wine. You bake the puffs in a ring, then pull them apart to serve. They're best served hot from the oven.

1 cup milk
¼ cup butter or margarine
½ teaspoon salt
   Dash pepper
1 cup all-purpose flour, unsifted
4 eggs
1 cup shredded Swiss cheese

Heat milk and butter in a 2-quart pan and add salt and pepper. Bring to full boil; add flour all at once, stirring over medium heat about 2 minutes or until mixture leaves sides of pan and forms a ball. Remove pan from heat; by hand, beat in eggs, one at a time, until mixture is smooth and well blended. Beat in ½ cup of the cheese.

Using about ¾ of the dough, make 7 equal mounds with an ice cream scoop or large spoon. On a greased baking sheet, place mounds of dough in a circle with each mound touching the next one. With remaining dough, place a small mound of dough on top of each larger mound. Sprinkle remaining ½ cup cheese over all.

Bake on center rack of a 375° oven for about 55 minutes or until puffs are lightly browned and crisp. Makes 7 puffs.

Buttermilk Scone Hearts

These fruit-laced, buttery, heart-shaped scones are sure to please any valentine on the morning of February 14. And they go together so quickly, you can sneak out of bed a little early and present them any day at breakfast as a surprise.

    3 cups all-purpose flour, unsifted
    ⅓ cup sugar
    2½ teaspoons baking powder
    ½ teaspoon soda
    ¾ teaspoon salt
    ¾ cup cold butter or margarine, cut in small
           pieces
    ¾ cup chopped pitted dates or currants
    1 teaspoon grated orange peel
    1 cup buttermilk
       About 1 tablespoon cream or milk
    ¼ teaspoon ground cinnamon mixed with 2
           tablespoons sugar

In a large bowl, stir together flour, sugar, baking powder, soda, and salt until thoroughly blended. Using a pastry blender or 2 knives, cut butter into flour mixture until it resembles coarse cornmeal; stir in dates and orange peel. Make a well in the center of the butter-flour mixture; add buttermilk all at once. Stir mixture with a fork until dough cleans the sides of the bowl.

With your hands, gather dough into a ball; turn out onto a lightly floured board. Roll or pat into a circle ½ inch thick. Using a 2½-inch heart (or other shape) cutter, cut into individual scones. Place 1½ inches apart on lightly greased baking sheets. Brush tops of scones with cream; sprinkle lightly with cinnamon-sugar mixture.

Bake in a 425° oven for 12 minutes or until tops are light brown. Serve warm. Makes about 18 scones.

Old-fashioned Cream Scones

There are many versions of scones, a British cousin of biscuits. These are rich and egg-flavored with a sugary top crust.

    2 cups all-purpose flour, unsifted
    3 teaspoons baking powder
    2 tablespoons sugar
    ½ teaspoon salt
    4 tablespoons butter or margarine
    2 eggs, beaten (reserve 1 tablespoon egg
           white for brushing on top)
    ⅓ cup whipping cream
    2 teaspoons sugar

In a large bowl stir together flour, baking powder, the 2 tablespoons sugar, and salt until thoroughly blended. Using a pastry blender or 2 knives, cut in the butter until mixture resembles fine crumbs. Stir in eggs and cream to make a stiff dough.

Turn out onto a lightly floured board and knead lightly until dough sticks together. Divide into two parts. Roll each part out to make a circle about 6 inches in diameter and about 1 inch thick. With a knife, cut each circle into 4 wedges. Arrange on an ungreased baking sheet about 1 inch apart. Brush tops of scones with the reserved egg white and sprinkle with the 2 teaspoons sugar.

Bake in a 400° oven for 15 minutes or until golden brown. Serve warm. Makes 8 scones.

Whole Wheat Scones

Made with stone-ground whole wheat flour, these scones have a wholesome quality and a crumbly texture similar to cornbread. Try them with a hearty breakfast on a cold winter's morning.

The raisin-studded millet variation following this recipe has a sweeter, lighter flavor. Look for millet meal at health food stores.

    2¼ cups stone-ground whole wheat flour,
           unsifted
    2 teaspoons baking powder
    ½ teaspoon *each* salt and soda
    3 tablespoons sugar
    ½ cup (¼ lb.) butter or margarine
    2 eggs, lightly beaten
    ⅓ cup milk

In a large bowl stir together whole wheat flour, baking powder, salt, soda, and 2 tablespoons of the sugar until thoroughly blended. Cut butter into chunks, add to bowl, and rub mixture together with your fingers until butter particles are no longer distinguishable. Measure 1 tablespoon of the beaten eggs and set aside. Stir milk into remaining egg until blended.

(Continued on next page)

With a fork, combine milk and egg mixture with flour mixture until evenly moistened.

With your hands pat dough (it is sticky) into a ball and place on a floured board. Knead dough lightly 2 or 3 turns, then place on a lightly greased baking sheet and pat into a smooth circle about 8 inches in diameter. Use a sharp knife dipped in flour to cut circle into 8 wedges; leave wedges in place. Brush with reserved egg and sprinkle with remaining 1 tablespoon sugar.

Bake in a 400° oven for 30 minutes or until golden brown and a skewer inserted in center of a wedge comes out clean. Cool about 5 minutes before serving. Makes 8 servings.

Millet Raisin Scones

Follow recipe for Whole Wheat Scones (preceding) with these changes: Omit whole wheat flour and add instead 1¼ cups **all-purpose flour** (unsifted) and 1 cup **millet meal**. Add ¾ cup **raisins** to dry ingredients. Substitute ¼ cup **sour cream** for milk.

Buttermilk Biscuits

Served hot from the oven, these old-fashioned biscuits are sure to be eaten quickly. They are as simple and good as the kind grandma used to bake.

- 2 cups all-purpose flour, unsifted
- 2½ teaspoons baking powder
- ¼ teaspoon salt
- ½ teaspoon soda
- 1 tablespoon sugar
- ⅓ cup butter, margarine, or shortening
- ¾ cup buttermilk

In a large bowl, stir together flour, baking powder, salt, soda, and sugar until thoroughly blended. Cut butter into chunks, add to bowl, and rub mixture together with your fingers until the largest pieces are no more than about ¼ inch in diameter. Pour in buttermilk and stir with a fork until dough sticks together and clings to the fork in a large lump. Turn dough onto a flour-dusted board, turning gently to coat all surfaces lightly with flour. Then knead, making about 10 turns.

Place dough in a lightly greased 9 or 10-inch round or square pan (a cake pan or frying pan that can go into the oven). Pat dough out evenly to fill pan. With a flour-dusted 2 to 3-inch round cutter, cut straight down through dough, then lift cutter straight up to make each biscuit; cut close together to make as many as possible. Leave scraps in place.

Bake in 400° oven for 15 to 20 minutes or until golden brown on top. Serve hot directly from the pan. Makes 9 to 16 biscuits.

Popovers

These beautiful creations are like fragile shells— nothing but crisp golden crusts and air. Lavish them with butter and preserves. You can bake them in your choice of containers: lightweight, shiny metal muffin pans, dark, heavy cast-iron popover pans, or ovenproof glass custard cups.

- 1 cup all-purpose flour (sift before measuring)
- ¼ teaspoon salt
- 1 teaspoon sugar (optional)
- 1 tablespoon melted butter or margarine, or salad oil
- 1 cup milk
- 2 large eggs

In a bowl, stir together flour, salt, and sugar (if used) until thoroughly blended. Add butter, milk, and eggs; beat until very smooth (about 2½ minutes), scraping bowl frequently with a rubber spatula. Fill greased ovenproof glass cups about half full with batter: twelve ⅓-cup size, ten ½-cup size, or eight or nine 6-ounce size.

For a richly browned shell with fairly moist interior, bake on center rack in a 400° oven for about 40 minutes or until well browned and firm to touch. For a lighter-colored popover, drier inside, bake in a 375° oven for 50 to 55 minutes. (Keep oven door closed; popovers may collapse if a draft of air hits them just as they are swelling above the cup, usually about ¾ of the way through the baking time.) Remove from pans and serve hot. Makes 8 to 12 popovers.

If you like the interior of popovers to be especially dry, loosen them from pan but leave sitting at an angle in cups; prick popovers' sides with a skewer and let stand in the turned-off oven, door slightly ajar, for 8 to 10 minutes.

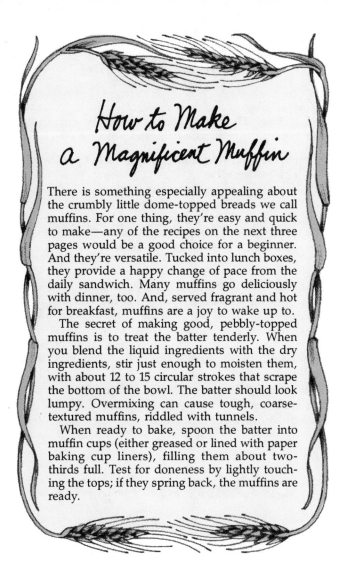

How to Make a Magnificent Muffin

There is something especially appealing about the crumbly little dome-topped breads we call muffins. For one thing, they're easy and quick to make—any of the recipes on the next three pages would be a good choice for a beginner. And they're versatile. Tucked into lunch boxes, they provide a happy change of pace from the daily sandwich. Many muffins go deliciously with dinner, too. And, served fragrant and hot for breakfast, muffins are a joy to wake up to.

The secret of making good, pebbly-topped muffins is to treat the batter tenderly. When you blend the liquid ingredients with the dry ingredients, stir just enough to moisten them, with about 12 to 15 circular strokes that scrape the bottom of the bowl. The batter should look lumpy. Overmixing can cause tough, coarse-textured muffins, riddled with tunnels.

When ready to bake, spoon the batter into muffin cups (either greased or lined with paper baking cup liners), filling them about two-thirds full. Test for doneness by lightly touching the tops; if they spring back, the muffins are ready.

Sweet Breakfast Muffins

Freshly baked hot muffins for breakfast can inspire the sleepiest person to arise in the morning. These fragrant little breads are also a good choice for a leisurely weekend brunch.

½ cup all-purpose flour, unsifted
¾ cup whole wheat flour, unsifted
2 teaspoons baking powder
½ teaspoon salt
1 egg
¼ cup melted butter or margarine, or salad oil
½ cup granulated sugar or firmly packed brown sugar (or 3 tablespoons honey)
½ cup milk

In a large bowl, stir together all-purpose flour, whole wheat flour, baking powder, and salt until thoroughly blended; make a well in the center. In a separate bowl, lightly beat egg; stir in melted butter, sugar or honey, and milk. Pour all at once into flour well. Stir just enough to moisten all the dry ingredients. Spoon batter into greased 2½-inch cups, filling each ⅔ full.

Bake in a 375° oven for about 25 minutes or until well browned and tops spring back when lightly touched. Makes about 9 muffins.

Cinnamon Nut-topped Muffins

Follow the recipe for Sweet Breakfast Muffins (left), and fill muffin cups. Combine in a bowl 2 tablespoons *each* packed **brown sugar** and chopped **walnuts or pecans** and ½ teaspoon ground **cinnamon.** Just before baking, sprinkle tops of muffins evenly with sugar-nut mixture. Makes about 9 muffins.

Fresh Apple Muffins

Follow the recipe for Sweet Breakfast Muffins (left), but add ½ teaspoon ground **cinnamon** to dry ingredients. Stir in 1 cup shredded (unpeeled) tart **apple** with the butter. Reduce milk to ⅓ cup. Makes about 10 muffins.

Cottage Cheese Muffins

Cottage cheese adds moistness to these whole grain muffins; cornmeal gives them an intriguingly crunchy texture.

1½ cups all-purpose flour, unsifted
½ cup buckwheat or whole wheat flour, unsifted
1 cup yellow cornmeal
4½ teaspoons baking powder
¼ teaspoon salt
3 tablespoons sugar
2 eggs
1 cup *each* small curd cottage cheese and buttermilk
⅓ cup salad oil

In a large bowl, stir together the all-purpose flour, buckwheat flour, cornmeal, baking powder, salt, and sugar until thoroughly blended. In a small bowl, beat eggs lightly; mix in cottage cheese, buttermilk, and oil. Make a well in center of flour mixture; add liquid ingredients. Stir with fork just to blend. Spoon into well-greased 2½-inch muffin cups, filling each ⅔ full.

Bake in a 400° oven for about 20 minutes or until browned and tops spring back when lightly touched. Makes 2 dozen muffins.

Ready-bake Bran Muffins

Freshly baked bran muffins for busy-morning break-fasts are a luxury easily achieved. These wholesome, almost cakelike muffins are made from a fruit-laced batter that keeps, ready to bake, in the refrigerator for about two weeks. You make the number of muffins you want, and they bake light and tender while the coffee brews and the bacon browns.

>3 **cups whole bran cereal**
>1 **cup boiling water**
>2 **eggs, lightly beaten**
>2 **cups buttermilk**
>½ **cup salad oil**
>1 **cup raisins, currants, chopped pitted**
>   **dates, or chopped pitted prunes**
>2½ **teaspoons soda**
>½ **teaspoon salt**
>1 **cup sugar**
>2½ **cups all-purpose flour, unsifted**

In a large bowl mix bran cereal with boiling water, stirring to moisten evenly. Set aside until cool, then add eggs, buttermilk, oil, and fruit and blend well. In a separate bowl, stir together soda, salt, sugar, and flour until thoroughly blended; then stir into bran mixture.

To store for later use, refrigerate batter in tightly covered container for as long as two weeks, and bake muffins at your convenience; stir batter to distribute fruit evenly before using. Spoon batter into greased 2½-inch muffin cups, filling each about ⅔ full.

Bake in a 425° oven for about 20 minutes or until tops spring back when lightly touched. Makes 2 to 2½ dozen muffins.

Oatmeal Muffins

Oatmeal gives these rather sweet muffins a distinc-tive texture. They are delicious plain or with butter and honey for breakfast or a midmorning snack.

>1 **cup regular or quick-cooking rolled oats**
>1 **cup buttermilk**
>1 **cup all-purpose flour, unsifted**
>½ **teaspoon** *each* **salt and soda**
>1½ **teaspoons baking powder**
>½ **cup butter or margarine, melted**
>½ **cup firmly packed brown sugar**
>1 **egg, beaten**

Combine oats and buttermilk; let stand for 30 min-utes. Stir together until thoroughly blended the flour, salt, soda, and baking powder. Add melted butter, sugar, and egg to oatmeal mixture and blend thor-oughly. Stir in dry ingredients just until blended. Spoon batter into greased 2½-inch muffin pans, filling each about ⅔ full.

Bake in a 350° oven for about 25 minutes or until browned and tops spring back when lightly touched. Makes 1 dozen muffins.

Gold Surprise Muffins

The surprising ingredient in these muffins is shred-ded carrot, contributing sweetness, moistness, and rich color.

>¼ **cup** *each* **butter or margarine and firmly**
>   **packed brown sugar**
>2 **eggs**
>1 **tablespoon** *each* **lemon juice and water**
>1 **cup finely shredded, lightly packed**
>   **carrots**
>1 **cup all-purpose flour, unsifted**
>2 **teaspoons baking powder**
>½ **teaspoon salt**
>¼ **teaspoon ground ginger**
>½ **to ¾ cup chopped almonds, pecans, or**
>   **walnuts (optional)**

Beat together butter and sugar until creamy. Add eggs and beat until light and fluffy. Stir in lemon juice, water, and shredded carrots; stir until well blended. In a separate bowl, combine flour with bak-ing powder, salt, and ginger; sift into carrot mixture. Add chopped nuts, if used. Stir just enough to mois-ten all the dry ingredients. Spoon batter into greased, 2½-inch muffin cups, filling each about ⅔ full.

Bake in a 400° oven for about 20 minutes or until tops spring back when lightly touched. Makes about 12 muffins.

Rhubarb Muffins

Moist, tender, and slightly tart, these muffins prove that rhubarb grows for more purposes than pie. You can serve them for breakfast or with afternoon tea.

1¼ cups firmly packed brown sugar
½ cup salad oil
1 egg
2 teaspoons vanilla
1 cup buttermilk
1½ cups diced rhubarb
½ cup chopped walnuts
2½ cups all-purpose flour, unsifted
1 teaspoon *each* soda and baking powder
½ teaspoon salt
Cinnamon topping (recipe follows)

In a large bowl, combine sugar, oil, egg, vanilla, and buttermilk; beat well. Stir in rhubarb and walnuts.

In a separate bowl, stir together flour, soda, baking powder, and salt until thoroughly blended. Stir dry ingredients into rhubarb mixture just until blended. Spoon batter into greased 2½-inch muffin cups, filling them about ⅔ full. Scatter cinnamon topping (recipe follows) over filled cups and press lightly into batter.

Bake in a 400° oven for 20 to 25 minutes or until muffins are delicately browned and tops spring back when lightly touched. Makes about 20 muffins.

Cinnamon topping. Combine 1 tablespoon melted **butter** or margarine with ⅓ cup **sugar** and 1 teaspoon ground **cinnamon**.

Whole Wheat Dinner Muffins

These robust, whole grain muffins are mildly sweet and can substitute nicely for bread at dinner. Serve them with fried chicken, roast pork or lamb, baked ham, and salads. *(Photograph on page 78.)*

Several equally wholesome and tasty variations follow this recipe.

1 cup all-purpose flour, unsifted
1 cup whole wheat flour, unsifted
¼ cup wheat germ
3 teaspoons baking powder
½ teaspoon salt
1 egg
¼ cup melted butter or margarine, or salad oil
¼ cup granulated sugar or firmly packed brown sugar (or 2 tablespoons honey)
1 cup milk

In a large bowl, stir together all-purpose flour, whole wheat flour, wheat germ, baking powder, and salt until thoroughly blended; make a well in the center. In a separate bowl, lightly beat egg; stir in melted butter, sugar or honey, and milk. Pour all at once into flour well. Stir just enough to moisten all the dry ingredients. Spoon batter into greased 2½-inch muffin cups, filling each ⅔ full.

Bake in a 375° oven for about 25 minutes or until well browned and tops spring back when lightly touched. Makes about 1 dozen.

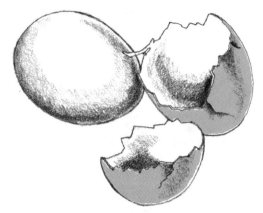

Bran Wheat Muffins

Follow recipe for Whole Wheat Dinner Muffins (left) but omit wheat germ and add ¾ cup whole **bran** cereal (not bran flakes) to dry ingredients.

Soy Muffins

Follow recipe for Whole Wheat Dinner Muffins (left), increasing **all-purpose flour** to 1½ cups. Omit whole wheat flour and wheat germ; add ½ cup **soy flour** (unsifted). They're particularly good made with honey.

Buckwheat Muffins

Follow recipe for Whole Wheat Dinner Muffins (left), but omit all-purpose flour. Increase **whole wheat flour** to 1½ cups and add ¼ cup **buckwheat flour** (both unsifted).

Buttermilk Oatmeal Muffins

Follow recipe for Whole Wheat Dinner Muffins (left), but omit wheat germ and add ½ cup rolled **oats**, (regular or quick-cooking) to dry ingredients. Decrease baking powder to 2 teaspoons and add ½ teaspoon **soda**. Omit milk and add 1 cup **buttermilk**.

Baking Mixes for the Camp Cook

A trick of the veteran camp cook is to blend and package a hearty baking mix before leaving home. Then, in camp, it's just a matter of adding milk or water to the basic mixture of whole grain flours, cereals, and leavening.

Here we suggest two such baking mixes. With either one, you can quickly turn out a variety of camp (or home) treats, using the recipes given here.

Soy-Wheat Baking Mix

Our first camp mix is a nourishing combination of whole wheat and soy flours enriched with wheat germ and brewer's yeast. Look for the soy flour and brewer's yeast at health food stores.

    1 cup whole wheat flour, unsifted
2½ cups unbleached white or all-purpose
        flour, unsifted
    ½ cup soy flour, unsifted
    ½ cup wheat germ
    6 teaspoons baking powder
1¼ teaspoons salt
    ⅔ cup low-fat dry milk product (made with
        cream)
    ½ cup sugar
    ¼ cup brewer's yeast

In a large bowl, thoroughly blend all ingredients. Package airtight in plastic bags or containers and store in a cool, dry place. Makes about 6 cups mix.

Sierra Camp Baking Mix

This second baking mix is a blend of three whole grain flours with crunchy cornmeal.

    2 cups whole wheat flour, unsifted
    1 cup *each* yellow cornmeal and rye flour,
        unsifted
    ½ cup soy flour
    6 tablespoons firmly packed brown sugar
3½ teaspoons baking powder
1¾ teaspoons *each* salt and soda

In a large bowl, thoroughly blend all ingredients. Package airtight in plastic bags or containers and store in a cool, dry place. Makes 5 cups mix.

Frying Pan Biscuits or Shortcakes. Combine 2 cups of either **baking mix** with ½ cup **milk or water** and 2 tablespoons **salad oil**; stir until thoroughly blended. Dust your hands with additional mix, shape dough into a ball, and divide it into 8 equal portions; pat each into a round about 2½ inches in diameter and about ½ inch thick.

Melt 1 tablespoon **butter** or margarine in a large heavy frying pan over low heat; add as many patted biscuits at a time as you can without crowding, and cook slowly, uncovered, for about 10 minutes until golden brown on bottom. Turn and cook for about 7 more minutes until other side is golden brown and biscuits are cooked through (break one to test). Repeat for any remaining biscuits, adding a little more butter to pan if needed.

Serve biscuits hot with butter and honey. Or, for shortcake, split and fill with sweetened fresh berries or cut-up canned fruit and top with a dollop of sour cream or canned imitation sour cream. Makes 8 biscuits or shortcakes.

Campsite Pancakes. In a bowl, stir together 1 cup of either **baking mix**, 1 **egg**, 2 tablespoons **salad oil**, and ½ cup **milk or water**. Melt about 1 tablespoon **butter** or margarine in a large heavy frying pan or griddle over medium heat; for each pancake, spoon about 3 tablespoons batter into pan and spread into a 3 to 4-inch circle. Cook until golden brown on bottom and bubbles break on top; turn and cook until other side is golden and pancakes are cooked through (break one to test). Serve with butter and honey or syrup. Makes 9 or 10 pancakes, 3 to 4 inches in diameter.

Trailside Crepes. In a bowl, beat together 1 cup of either **baking mix**, 2 **eggs**, and 1 cup **milk or water** until smooth. Heat about ¼ teaspoon **butter** or margarine in a small heavy frying pan or crepe pan (6 to 6½ inches in diameter) over medium heat. At once pour in about 1½ tablespoons batter, quickly tilting pan so batter flows over entire flat surface. Cook until surface appears dry and edge is lightly browned. With a wide spatula, turn and brown other side. Turn out of pan onto a plate. Repeat for each crepe, stacking them.

To serve, spoon sweetened fresh berries or cut-up canned fruit down middle of each, then roll and top with sour cream or canned imitation sour cream. Makes about 1½ dozen crepes.

Dutch Oven Dumplings. About 20 minutes before your favorite camp stew is ready to serve, stir together 1 cup of either **baking mix**, 1 **egg**, ⅓ cup **milk or water**, and 1 tablespoon **freeze-dried chives** until thoroughly blended. Drop in 6 large mounds on top of simmering stew. Cover and let simmer for 15 minutes without lifting lid; dumplings should be dry on top and cooked through when slashed. Makes 6 servings.

Index

Metric Conversion Table

To change	To	Multiply By
ounces (oz.)	grams (g)	28
pounds (lb.)	kilograms (kg)	0.45
teaspoons	milliliters (ml)	5
tablespoons	milliliters (ml)	15
fluid ounces (oz.)	milliliters (ml)	30
cups	liters (l)	0.24
pints (pt.)	liters (l)	0.47
quarts (qt.)	liters (l)	0.95
gallons (gal.)	liters (l)	3.8
Fahrenheit temperature (°F)	*Celsius temperature (°C)*	*5/9 after subtracting 32*